Simple Steps

To A

Better Life

By: Sandra Williams

Simple Steps To A Better Life

Copyright © 2016 by Sandra Williams
All rights reserved. No part of this publication may be reproduced, stored in a retrieval system, or transmitted in any form by any means, mechanical, electronic, recording, photocopying or otherwise without prior written permission from the author.
The author would like to acknowledge the following publications:
Scripture quotations marked NLT are taken from the Holy Bible, New Living Translation, copyright 1996, 2004. Used by permission of Tyndale House Publishers, Inc., Wheaton, Illinois 60189. All rights reserved.
Scripture taken from *The Message*. Copyright © 1993, 1994, 1995, 1996, 2000, 2001, 2002. Used by permission of NavPress Publishing Group.
Scripture taken from the New King James Version. Copyright © 1982 by Thomas Nelson, Inc. Used by permission. All rights reserved.

ISBN 978-0-9977450-0-9

Dedicated to:

My Children, Grandchildren,

Great Grandchildren

And The

Generations That Follow

After

Simple Steps To A Better Life

ACKNOWLEDGMENTS

I would like to thank God for the many gifts He has given me, the friendship, love, understanding, forgiveness and all the wonderful blessings He has bestowed on our family. I want to thank all my family, friends and acquaintances for the parts they played in my life and the experiences from each that has made me into who I am today. I want to thank my grandmother Alice Porcello for her love and support throughout my life, for her kind words and encouragement in anything I attempted to do. Many thanks to Henry, my husband and friend for over 30 years, for all the support, encouragement and love he has shown me through the years, and our boys, Jonathan, Michael, Henry Jr. and Kyle for being so understanding throughout their lives with all the sometimes very difficult times throughout our lives. We can definitely say that we are blessed by God and there is no doubt of His working throughout our family. He has brought us through many an ordeal and to many peoples amazement we are still standing and doing better than ever. God is faithful and He has never let us down. I also wish to thank all our family and friends throughout my life and the many contributions they have made. May God bless each and every one of you and the many preachers and teachers for the diligence you have shown in your effort to "get the gospel out". May you be blessed through your reading.

Simple Steps To A Better Life

PREFACE

My children, daughters-in-law, grandchildren and great-grandchildren to come, I have seen and been through a lot in my life, as so shall you. God has always been with me, as He is with each of you. I have always had a fascination about my relatives before me and what their lives were like. This book does not so much have to do with the daily routine and material status of life as the world looks at it, but it does deal greatly with the inner life, the real life, the spoken and unspoken actions of life, the meaning of life and who you are, where you have come from, how to conduct yourself, how to steer clear from the pitfalls that will come and try to get you to give up, cave in and quit if at all possible.

The first thing I want you to know is that you are a spirit, (created in Gods own image) you possess a soul (made up of your mind, will and emotions) and you live in a body (the body is what allows you to have dominion (or rule) on this earth). I am writing this to you, my family and descendants for the simple fact that the world is more unstable than ever and there are so many deceptions out there. I want you to have a place to go to, to be able to put stock in a place of your own to know your family history.

Our heritage is a Christian one. We are believers all at varying degrees and in different stages in our walk. We are each at different levels, but none the less on the way to fulfilling Gods plan for us. We believe that God is the creator of all things and we are made in His image. We believe the "whole" Bible. We may not have some things it speaks of in full use, but we believe if God said it in His word, then it is true and that anything we may not understand or that goes against the circumstances we may be experiencing does not make the Bible untrue, it simply means that we need to take dominion over our circumstance and grow to the place where circumstances no longer have dominion over us. I want to thank God for giving us a strong heritage. He has been good to us. This does not mean that we have come through life unscathed; it means He has mercy on us to endure and grow through and in spite of our difficulties. He has given me wisdom I want to pass on to you. Teach it to your children and your children's children.

    Just to set the record straight, Jesus is the answer and holds every key you need to unlock fullness, peace, joy and love in your life. Without acceptance of Jesus you will never know true "shalom" (a state of being which constitutes fullness, wholeness, nothing missing and nothing broken). Shalom is a state of being only true believers will ever be able to live in continuously throughout their entire life and circumstances cannot take this wholeness from you.

    God has a full, rich life ahead for you and the more you come to know Him and His ways and the closer you are to Him the more you will see His hand at work in your life and your life will be very complete, rich and satisfying beyond your wildest dreams.

My prayer for you is that you walk with God more closely than past generations and live the life of excellence that God has so richly blessed you with. May you cherish every moment of your life and cherish all the love in your life and reach out to bestow the gifts God has given you to help others along the way with their relationship with God.

May you know the exceedingly great measure of His love for you, a love without end and a love that will never die.

Chapter One

Life Cycles

Life is a series of events, the same cycle tends to hold true from generation to generation, unless someone breaks the cycle. This is truly a hard task, for we are creatures of habit and usually tend toward the familiar because that is what we are used to and comfortable with. There is nothing wrong with this as long as they are good habits, solid and healthy for a fulfilling life. Unfortunately, there are things that are passed down that are not good for us as well. Some people call these generational curses. These curses came about through what I call "knowing better, but not doing better". Choosing to do wrong repeatedly and going against your knowledge of the right thing to do in a circumstance (going against what you know God wants you to do) will always turn out bad for you, and not only for you but for the next generations after you according to the word of God. Not all past generations or even we now, have it so together that there is no room for improvement, but to do wrong repeatedly and to continue to go against your spirit (some may call it their conscience) and better judgment will always turn out bad for you. It will take you down a path you don't want to be on and you will not be able to possess fullness of life and joy as you should because those wrong choices will take you somewhere you don't want to be, a place where you will end up feeling empty. Whenever you feel this way then you have to re-evaluate yourself, find the errors in judgment you have made and correct them – by all means, do not continue in them! If you want a change in your life, then make a change in your thinking, choices and actions.

We need to look at our lives constantly and critique the life we now live and make solid decisions to do better, to come up higher to a greater quality of life. We often forget that life is a gift. It isn't about all the things materially you have acquired. It isn't about your home or your job. It is about love and the lives you touch as you live.

Everyone has a sphere of influence, everyone. There is not a person alive who has no effect on this world, on his or her family and friends, acquaintances, and strangers alike. Many people don't even realize what a difference they make when just offering a kind smile, a consideration or a courtesy to another. Whether you know them or not, a kind and tenderhearted person can touch and break through many barriers. I know this is not the norm for our day and age. It's a very rare thing to find someone who isn't so absorbed in themselves and their own gain that they would want to and even require themselves to have a life that reaches beyond its own interests and reaches out to another, especially when there is no material benefit to do so.

Simple Steps To A Better Life

There are however many intangible benefits and a great inner satisfaction, a sense of accomplishment, a wonderful strength of usefulness when you put yourself aside to help another along in their journey. Don't get me wrong, the proper priorities make or break a life. God and your personal relationship with him should always come first (I'm not talking church work, I am talking personal relationship) and He should always be the center of your life. Second, your spouse and the commitment you have made to them. The third priority should be your immediate family, your children, parents and those others closest in your life. After these others comes your job. Some forget that the job and the money your work creates are solely for the benefit of the family. When the job has taken place of the family position then the purpose for working has changed and something is bound to be lost in the delicate balance of life. Some allow the job to take first place before God, spouse, children and other ones we are to love. Do not allow yourself to fall into this trap. Yes, the world revolves around money and money is necessary for survival and pleasures, but never give money and the love of money precedence over your family needs.

Do not neglect your family to make money. There will always be money to be made, but the individuals that make up your family may not always be there. One day, we all will leave this earth and just because you may have money in the bank it will not satisfy the loss of not being there for the person you love who needed you and now is gone.

Simple Steps To A Better Life

Since we are creatures of habit, we need to use the Word of God as our reference and line up our thoughts, actions and habits according to the Word of God and the finished work of Jesus. By doing this and teaching our children to do the same we will be creating new habits and lifestyles that will continue for generations to come that will bring blessing, joy, peace and greater love for, not only ourselves but also for all those our lives touch.

Passing down good to our children will give them greater knowledge toward living the Blessed Life. A life where they know their dominion, authority and place in Christ and have control in every area as God designed for us to walk in. (Read *Galatians 3, Luke 10:19-20, Colossians 2:2-7)*.

Chapter Two

Keep Balance

Everything requires balance. Without balance families fall apart, people divorce and people begin not to care about each other. They think "What benefit is it to me?", "I'm not going to gain anything by doing this." Then before you know it they are just as selfish as the next and there is no longer a difference they can make in a life, none other than their own, they won't give of themselves to make that difference that only they can make. Balance is a key ingredient in life. Without it you tend to sway from one extreme to the other opposite extreme. Life is a very delicate balance between set priorities, wants, needs and your attention. Many things will demand your time and you must have your priorities to be able to keep all of life and its demands in their proper place. Jobs will try to pressure you to give more to them and leave your family's needs to another, but you must not give in to demands above their priority.

Your first priority must always be God and your relationship with Him. We all have got to come to the point of knowledge that without Him we are nothing more than ashes. He is the one that gives us our every breath. He is the one who made us. He is the one who has our every hair numbered. He is our protector and provider. He is the one who gives us mercy when we do wrong and provides a way out of every trap that has been set to entangle us. He is the one who tells us things before they happen and warns us about things that we have to go through. God is the one who gives us peace in the midst of the storm so we can handle the circumstance in a favorable way. God is all in all and Lord of all, even of those who won't acknowledge Him. Your relationship with Him must be first, above all others. Without God in his proper place you will never be able to ascertain appropriate balance throughout the rest of your life and all its demands.

      Your second priority (if married) is your spouse. I pray that you married this person with Gods approval and that you spoke with Him and listened to Him rather than following after your own lusts. Regardless, if you are married now, you must give your spouse top worldly priority. When you married and previously (I hope) you had discussions of what each expected of the other, you pledged your love and made vows before God in accordance to things you would fulfill to that person. Any vows made must always be upheld. God hates divorce and it seems that anything God disapproves of is what the world is doing. I am not saying that at times you won't have to go into "tough love" mode, what I am saying is that when you marry you are making a "forever" commitment. Marriage should not be entered into lightly and the vows you make to each other should not be broken under any circumstances. I always tell you, my children, that even when you marry with God's blessing it is a tough road, very hard at times, so be picky, very picky and be sure that God wants this person for you because once you make the commitment, your view should be, that it is forever. We don't believe in divorce although we have had divorces in our family, we do all we can to follow God's leading in this very important decision. God has the perfect person picked out for you and you need to know that you know, this is Gods choice for you. If you are divorced, learn from your mistakes, repent, forgive your ex-spouse and receive God's forgiveness for yourself. This is not an unpardonable sin. God still loves you deeply and if you allow Him, He will use you in a mighty way.

Your third priority needs to be your family, children, parents, etc. Your family is the people who will be there for you even when you mess up. They are going to be the ones that you should be able to call for anything and they are there for you even if it is only to talk. They are the ones you can turn to and because of their love for you they will be honest with you, they should help to instruct, teach and correct you. Some of my "family" is just super close friends that I know will always be there for me. When the rest of my life isn't going to well my family is always there to encourage and advise me and are the ones who help me to regroup and refocus on God. They pray for me and with me when I can't seem to talk to God myself. "Family" is very important not to sever ties completely from. I have some I only talk to every ten years or so but yet even after all that time it is as if it were only yesterday we spoke last. Remember that even those family members who have wrong attitudes like those that say "sounds like a personal problem" or "if you're going to be dumb you better be tough" that the ties with them should not be severed either because God can use you to teach them what love is or they may be in a place in their lives that you have not come into yet and their words, if you leave them on a back burner, may one day make sense to you as you mature yourself. Don't be too quick to judge, you may find later in life that their theory or words make sense to you now that you are in a new place in life yourself and always forgive their inadequacies when they simply just can't help you. Don't hold things against others. Chalk it up as a lesson learned and move on.

      You are a tool for God to use to help others come to know God as we know Him. Don't allow your family to be cut off and not see living truth in your life. Putting up with wrong actions and responses on occasion is part of our suffering, but it is also what makes us aware of how to pray for them. As they see our response to difficult situations, then you may have just opened a door for God to work within them to change their actions and responses. Most people will watch and if they see that our actions have favorable results then they will try to apply those same principles and actions to their lives to obtain favorable results for themselves and their situation. We never know why certain things happen, but we do know that God is in control and His plan will be fulfilled.

Your next priority should be your job. Whether you work inside the home, outside the home or both, all jobs are equally important. The stay at home mom is just as important as the husband who brings home the money. Everyone should do their part around the home. I was a stay at home mom for 16 years. I made sure there was food in the house and that everyone had clothes to wear and that the house wasn't a total disaster. I always enjoyed doing my wifely home maker duties; I received real pleasure and satisfaction from being home with you, my children, and raising you. I was happy to be able to instill in you my values, beliefs and morals. I believe I did my job well according to the bibles, "train up a child in the way he should go: and when he is old, he will not depart from it". (King James Version)

Now my husband on the other hand, due to an injury, was home for about a month when we only had one child at home. His eyes were opened to what it was to be home all day with a toddler. He commended me for my tolerance and endurance and even went back to work before time because it was much harder and more to deal with than he realized. I thank God for the experience because it defiantly gave him a sense of appreciation for what I did around the home and with our children (we have four boys).

Simple Steps To A Better Life

Gods plan is that the man be the provider for the family. I understand that many women have to work as well to make ends meet, but then if the provision of money is a shared responsibility then the work around the home should be divided equally as well. Although dad may be the sole provider of the home, that is no excuse not to spend quality time with his children daily. Remember balance is the key to life.

Balance is not something that comes over night. It takes a lot of time and purposed decisions to put balance in place and keep it in place. As with all things in life, you must learn to adjust and adapt easily to situations beyond your control. As you go through life you will notice (if you are watching), that you are not living in perfect balance but you must wholeheartedly believe you are doing the best you can for where you are at this point in your life and continually strive for better. Make those small adjustments to your life daily and continue in them, eventually they will become part of you and your routine. All those little changes toward balancing out your life will pay off and when you look at how far you have progressed toward the goal of balance you will be pleasantly amazed at how far your efforts have brought you!

I believe that you have to accept where you are and as long as you are doing the best you can continuously, prayerfully and with proper motive, that God will work out all the rest. Definitely, keeping balance in your life in all things is, (as with many things in life), a constant area to watch and do your best to keep in tune with Gods leading and direction.

Sometimes we just have to sit back and do the best we can to enjoy where we are, on the way to where we are going. This is easier said than done but with a right attitude you can enjoy your life here and now, although the day may not hold what you expected.

With God leading and guiding us by the Word and Holy Spirit, we will be able to maintain balance in our life. Holy Spirit will keep us in all Gods ways provided we are listening and will do as he tells us.

God says he has an appointed time for every purpose under Heaven (*Ecclesiastes 3*). There may be times that we have to put more time and effort into certain areas for a period, like starting a new business or something of the like, but you should watch and adjust all areas as needed based on need and priority.

If a choice of working extra hours or being home has become a struggle or is causing strife then do what is required to keep the home happy and strife and struggle out of your life. God has no part in contention. God is all about harmony and unity in Christ.

Be sure you communicate openly and without attitude whatever your feelings and be respectful to listen and understand others. Your main goal is to keep balance and home life well and good. We don't want to give the devil place or room to work by being upset with anyone and thinking wrong thoughts ourselves.

Simple Steps To A Better Life

Proper knowledge of others feelings can help in keeping balance. We don't want to shut down communications or cause strife. We must do our best to keep peace. Keep increasing in wisdom, knowledge and in favor with God and man. You will find Holy Spirit can keep you in perfect balance and harmony. To accomplish this you must be willing to lay down pride and self in order to hear Holy Spirit and not over-ride him with your own thoughts and feelings.

I can do all things through Christ who strengthens me. Believe it and speak it often, especially when you want to rise up rather than keep a servant attitude as Jesus carried. Read *Philippians.*

Chapter Three
Enjoy Life

This may be one of the hardest things that you ever do. There are so many wrong thoughts that attack us and if we listen to them and go with them, they will cause us to think differently and steal our joy. God has called us to enjoy life. "Lighten up and live" is a statement that always stands out to me. I am a very serious person, too serious sometimes. Don't take what I'm saying and twist it around to suit you. I am not saying do whatever feels good. I am saying that through knowing God you are given a gift of joy and that joy is "the joy of the Lord which is your strength". You will be attacked in this area as well upon occasion throughout your life. All kinds of things will be thrown at you to get you off balance and they have come for one purpose, to steal your joy. Circumstances, situations, thoughts, complications, health issues, you name it. There are so many things that happen through the course of a life that their main purpose is to steal your joy, to make you become weak and cause you to give up, cave in and quit and not only will you be bombarded with this but also with all types of temptations. There will come a time when you feel so worn out, but let me tell you; find your joy, get in the word, fill yourself with right thinking and right attitudes, stand and never give up. God is able to do exceedingly abundantly above all you could ask or think, but I'm sure those aren't the thoughts you will be having while you go through this stage, that is why we have to fill our minds with proper thoughts and attitudes. You may come to a place where you have to fight to keep any and all things that pertain to life and godliness in control. At times it will seem that all things are against you, but always remember that "things are not as they appear" and that "this to will pass". Everything, no matter how hopeless things may appear, with God all things are possible and all things will work out for the good of those that love God and keep and follow in His ways.

    We who follow after him have an invisible protective shield. God said He will not allow more than we can bear, so if life seems unbearable then it is time to dig a little deeper because there must be more strength in you than you realize. God says in our weakness He will show Himself strong. Once again, you can be used in this trial as a tool for God to touch people around you and to show His strength through your response to the "storms" of your life. Again, we are used in His master plan to show others who don't know Him the strength that knowing Him has given us and brought us through these rough patches in life. As long as you can find good in all things and you refuse to be controlled by thoughts against God and his word then you will be able to keep your joy.

    With God all things are "yea". God wants you to be a positive person. He doesn't want us to be unbelieving, negative people. He wants us to know who we are in Christ and be full of faith and positive confessions. After all, "your tongue is the rudder" and sets the course of your life, and "as a man believes in his heart so is he" or "you'll have what you say".

    I am able to find joy in knowing that God is in control of all things concerning me because I made Jesus my Lord and Savior. I find joy knowing that He has already accomplished and given to me all things pertaining to life and godliness. I have joy in knowing I don't have to punish myself for my mistakes, that I am able to go to Him and repent (turn away from and ask forgiveness for, change my mind about) and that He hears my prayers. I find joy knowing I can intercede for others. I can pray for them, ask they come to repentance for them, stand in the gap for them and I know that God hears my prayers and that through my faith in those prayers and my faith in Gods ability, the person I stand in the gap for will not be condemned. There are many reasons to have joy. The more you look the more you will find.

    The more you come to know God and His love for you the more joy will rise within you. There is a place where it feels like you are overflowing in joy and that joy, that gift from God cannot be compared to. It is better than anything you may try to compare it to on this earth.

Truly you will feel that "your cup (heart) is running over" not only with joy but with love, because after all God is love and you cannot have love or talk about love without God because he is the fullness of love. When you want to know about something, go to the source.

God can teach you about love better than anyone or anything else because He is Love. He doesn't possess it. He IS it. Now, there is a concept for you to try and take hold of! Wherever you find love you have found God. Now that is a happy thought!! I am not talking lust or an emotion based on feelings. I am talking true love.

The bottom line is that you need to live and walk in this gift of joy God has given you. If you allow this gift to be stolen by circumstances and other things in the events of life that are unpleasant then you will have allowed yourself to have become vulnerable and open to further attack until the door is open so wide you will want to give up, cave in or quit. This is what the plan of attack is against you. If you can be convinced that you are defeated, or that "things will never change" then you will not be able to be used by God in the fullness that He desires of you and then you are allowing (through your own deception) to be swayed by the thief who comes only to kill, steal and destroy your life.

Understand this; he cares nothing for you other than that you are out of commission and out of his way.

If you are on the road of least resistance and life doesn't give you the fullness and satisfaction that you crave, then you really need to look at the life you are living and judge yourself if you are living with Gods' purpose for your life and your relationship with Him is in first priority.

A life lacking God is a life wanting and unfulfilled. This is no way to live, unsatisfied and lonely although you may have a whole congregation around you. Living, knowing, although you may have it all, all the material desires a person could want, you still are greatly aware that something is missing, there is a "hole" that nothing in this world can fill. That "hole" came through the fall of man and it will never be filled until you have accepted Christ as your Lord and Savior and give yourself fully to Him.

It tends that when people feel this they start to look at fleshy ways to try and fix this. Some do body work, boob jobs, tummy tucks and the like. Others start looking for things they think will bring them pleasure outside the home and become a run around. When they are all done they find that all that didn't help them "feel better" about themselves or their lives. All they accomplished was more problems, they usually wind up divorced, their kids become a mess, confusion has taken over and now not only they are a mess but they have made their whole family a mess as well.

God will meet you where you are. He accepts you as you are. There is nothing that you have ever done that the blood of Jesus cannot cleanse. Just accept Him and believe what He has done for you.

Simple Steps To A Better Life

He will meet you where you are and pick up all your pieces and help you fix them one by one, until one day down the road somewhere you will look back and see just how far He has brought you.

This is the foundation of our receiving the gift of joy that God has laid aside waiting for us to accept. God has many gifts for us to receive; they all start with the gift of salvation. Once you have received this gift then, at that same moment all the other gifts are waiting for you to learn how to lay hold of and then put them to use. There is nothing that does not belong to you once you receive the gift of salvation. Although there are some gifts that you will be unable to use until a certain maturity level, the same with all parents who care for their children. You wouldn't give your toddler the keys to your car and let them drive off in it knowing it would hurt them, maybe even kill them. How much more the Father of Love would not allow us access to certain things until we have reached a place of maturity to be able to handle it in a way where we won't be hurt by it.

God has set aside for each of us many gifts. Once God has revealed to you all He has waiting for you, you will develop such a sense of expectation and looking to what lies ahead for you, as you press toward the mark and move toward the prize of the high calling to know God and show yourself faithful these many delightful gifts will be given to you.

Start where you are and move forward to attain all God has for you and the farther you follow God, the more that you will be trusted with, as you continue to show yourself faithful and mature in the grace and mercy of God.

Romans 5:3-5 **We can rejoice, too, when we run into problems and trials, for we know that they are good for us— they help us learn to endure. And endurance develops strength of character in us, and character strengthens our confident expectation of salvation. And this expectation will not disappoint us. For we know how dearly God loves us, because he has given us the Holy Spirit to fill our hearts with his love. (NLT)**

    JOY, one of Gods many great gifts to us. From it we have strength because we know our Fathers great love for us. Read *John 10:10* in the amplified version. God wants us in abundance, in all things. No lack, not just enough, but even more. Exceedingly abundantly above all we can ask or think. We love Him because He first loved us. We believe in Him and we are filled with joy unspeakable and full of glory even the salvation of our soul (see *1 Peter 1:8-9)*.

    Joy is different from happiness. Joy has nothing to do with the natural or circumstances all being perfect. Joy has everything to do with the inner man, the spirit man, and the real you, the reborn you knowing and communing with God by means of Holy Spirit.

    God fills us with all joy and peace, as we trust in him. He wants us to overflow with hope, a work done by the Holy Spirit as we trust (see *Romans 15:13)*.

    1 Timothy 6:17 tells us that God richly provides us with everything for our enjoyment. Many *Psalms* tell us to rejoice in the Lord. As we act on the Word of God by faith, even if we "aren't feeling it" our faith mixed with the word and our believing will open the door for joy to rise up within us. Whether rejoicing through reading, singing or prayer joy will come and God wants your joy to be full measure, complete and overflowing.

      After all God has done for us, how could we not be full of joy? We don't have to live under the curse! Jesus died in our place so we can live and through Him we are joint heirs to ALL Gods promises! When we keep our mind on all we've been given it is impossible not to rejoice and fill with joy.

Chapter Four
Character and Integrity

Read *James 1:2-4* it says, whenever trouble comes your way to let it be an opportunity for joy because it tests your faith and your endurance has a chance to grow. So let it grow because when your endurance is fully developed, you will be strong in character, lacking nothing and ready for anything. **(NLT)**

God, our creator, created not only us but the whole system of family. He created the first family and He knows the proper way to keep it all in balance and proper perspective. Yes, there are many times in our lives that we are out of balance, it has happened to us all. There are none who have never been out of proper balance in some point and time in their life. What we do, with what we have done and learned is what will be the judge of our character and what we will become.

Character is developed through your responses to all the different situations that you go through in your life. A good character is developed through making one right and good decision after another, and even when an error in judgment is made it is quickly changed, learned from and watched after closely so as not to make the same mistake again. A person of good character is quick to learn and ever watching for any indiscretions that could later lead to wrong results. We should always be watching and calculate the end product of our choices. Ask yourself, "Is this going to take me toward my goal of pleasing God, or will it take me away from the path that I want to walk down?" Ask yourself, "Will this choice please God?"

As long as we are watching ourselves and discerning our thoughts and intentions, and we repeatedly chose to do what we believe in our heart is the thing that is going to please our Creator, then even if we do mess up or miss the mark unintentionally God will work it all out and fix it because He knows our heart. You can be sure that you will never be able to play "games" with God. He knows all things and He knows each of us better than we know ourselves. With this fact in mind, you might as well be "real" with God, because if you really think you are fooling Him then you are the greatest fool of all. You will never "get over on" or "play" Him. Your character is your most important asset. Your word is the only credible part of your life that really matters. Having integrity is going to be your toughest challenge until it is mastered.

Integrity comes with good character. Integrity is doing what you say. A person with integrity, you can be rest assured that whatever they tell you they are going to do, they will do it. A person of integrity will never give you cause to question, "Do you really think they will?" You will know that they will and that you can count on them, otherwise they would not have made the commitment.

A person of integrity knows that every word they speak leads their life down a path and that they will have what they say. They are slow to speak and quick to listen. They make every decision carefully and weigh all matters fully. They have goals and make a plan to attain those goals, then most of all; they stick to that plan as closely as possible. Yes, there are times when things come up and the plan may have to be shifted or altered, but they adapt easily and proceed to the destination even with all the situations that come their way.

I tend to think that a person with integrity may have more trouble verbally committing to something than someone who does not value their words. I tend to see more responses in the line of "we will see" and "let's see how it plays out". Sometimes responses of this manner are frustrating to the one wanting the commitment but I tend to think that it is sometimes better to leave things in the air than to commit and then not follow through.

Now again, you don't want to get out of balance and never commit to anything. To have no sense of duty is not the answer either, but that delicate balance must be found. You cannot be at church every time the doors are open and neglect the family who is the higher priority, but yet you should not neglect the participation needed in the church totally either.

I believe we each have to pray and wait for God to tell us individually what He wants us to do. I believe that after you have prayed for God to give you a heart after His heart and to give you the desires of His heart, that you will know the desire He has for you because it will be your own heart's desire.

Character and integrity are both very important elements of a Christian. When Christians do not have these qualities yet they profess religion the world then criticizes all Christians. This is one of the main things that have given Christians a bad name. The world does not know the difference between religion and relationship with God. There is a huge difference. This you will come to see for yourself as you develop your own relationship with God. He will open your eyes to the true and the false concepts that are taught.

Integrity is not only the quality of being honest and having strong moral principles, being truthful and trustworthy, but it also has another side. Integrity is also the state of being whole and undivided, having unity, cohesion, togetherness and harmonious. It is important that we keep all division out. A house divided against itself cannot stand. Read *Mark 3:24-26*. Division brings an end. God is into multiplication and growth.

Chapter Five
Who are you?

  Our lives are a series of events and it is what we choose to do with these things that mold us into who we are. Are you a disciplined person, able to overcome all your fleshy desires? Do you have yourself so in order that you never lose your temper? Or never yell? Or never react in a negative way? Do you always respond with love and understanding?

  Your response will gauge where you are on a personal level. The more explosive you are the more selfish you are. Explosive people don't take the time to think or consider another. Explosive people are only concerned with their train of thought, their feelings, and their life. They won't take the time to consider another or where they are coming from and they certainly will not ask or care about another, their feelings, or any other part of rudimentary life unless of course there is some benefit to them in the pretense. You will find many people who fit this category throughout your life.

  Always remember to do your best at all you do, and relationships with other people are the core of life. You be good to others even when they don't deserve it and aren't good to you. You be the bigger person and let go of all offenses. When you hold something against another, you are the person who is being hurt. The other person neither cares nor consumes themselves with your problem. Their life goes on and you are holding on to something that will hurt you.

Holding offenses will cause deep roots to bitterness and jealousy. These ingredients are never healthy for any person. One of the best ways to be sure not to be led by your feelings is to stay in the word of God. Be sure you judge yourself against the word and when you find things out of line within yourself repent (change your mind to agree with the Word) immediately and ask God to rip out the "sin" from its roots.

As you go through the bible, be sure to line yourself up with what God says about you. One of the most important things you will ever do is learn who you are in Christ. Once you have learned what Christ has done for you and how God sees you, you will be able to judge rightly the many thoughts that come to you telling you how bad you are and worthless. These things may have been true "back in the day" but you are no longer that person, the moment you accepted Jesus as your Lord and Savior, old things were washed away by the blood He shed for you and Behold, all things became new and if things are brought to your attention that you shouldn't be doing now, quickly repent and believe that God has forgiven you. Truly He has!

When God looks at you He sees the innocent blood of Jesus that was poured over you the day you accepted Christ into your life. You are covered in the blood that is without sin, spotless and without blemish. When the accuser comes, Jesus defends your life. There is nothing in this world that will get you forgiven and into Heaven other than the blood of Jesus. There are no great works or sacrifices or anything else that has the value and covering as the blood has. Without it you will surely perish. With it you are unstoppable. There is nothing that can hold you back from being an over comer in life other than yourself. Only you will have the power to choose to be defeated. Otherwise there is nothing in this world that can defeat you unless you choose to let it.

Do you know you are the righteousness of God? If you have accepted Christ you are! It was one of the many gifts given to you at the new birth. It has nothing to do with you. It doesn't matter if you feel like it or not. It doesn't matter how many times you have messed up. None of that has anything to do with anything! It is a gift and you can possess it and live with it and enjoy the presence of this awesome gift, but first you must accept and believe it. God said it in His word along with many other gifts you don't even know you possess so it is still in the closet of your heart all wrapped up just waiting for you to come and get it, unwrap it and embrace it.

All these lovely things that God has given to you and you have never even attempted to find out all you were given or grow in God so you could come to the place of knowledge, wisdom and understanding so you could use these gifts to your greatest benefit, or for some, use them and receive any benefit.

Simple Steps To A Better Life

Some don't even know all they possess, and as with anything that we have and never use or don't even realize we have, then we totally wind up struggling through and many times feeling we have had little or no victory.

I really hope you see now why it is so important to get into your bible and learn of Him and all He died to give you. He has called you for a special purpose and He has equipped you to carry out His wishes, but you need to run through the equipment list and make sure you know what you have and the proper way to use it. The wisdom and understanding of this is relevant to whether you will live a successful life or a defeated life. It really is time for you to dig in and learn in its fullness WHO YOU ARE IN CHRIST. It makes a world of difference each and every day. I'd rather know what I have and how to use it rather than be beat up and whipped, especially when there was no reason for it to have to be that way, other than sheer laziness and stupidity on my part because I wouldn't give it its proper place in my priorities or in my life.

Get in the bible and find out who you are and what you have been given. Mature in God's word so you can un-wrap all the gifts He has, just waiting for you. I promise, you will lose any self-esteem issues that you may have, once you know and believe what the blood of Jesus has given you.

To start you out, search the scriptures. Find all the verses that say, "In Him", "In whom", and "In Christ" (I use the King James Version) – these scriptures tell you who you are and what you have been given through the shed blood. Getting in the Word is the process of renewing your mind to the word. Remember it doesn't matter how you feel. It matters what you believe.

1 Peter 1:8-9 says, **Whom having not seen, ye love; in whom, though now ye see him not, yet believing, ye rejoice with joy unspeakable and full of glory: Receiving the end of your faith, even the salvation of your souls.** (KJV)

The above tells you through accepting and believing in Him, you rejoice, have joy unspeakable, you're full of glory and the salvation of your soul. According to this you have what is necessary, and should be, happy, full of praise, honor and thankfulness. If this does not describe you then you have yet another gift from God that you need to accept, claim and lay hold of, until you possess your gift and the evidence of its acceptance is flowing from you.

At some point you are going to have to make the decision to stop believing the lies of the enemy and chose to believe the Word and what God your creator, has to say about you. Now is a good time to believe. Jesus died for you and if you have accepted him as Lord and Savior, you are his brother. You are fearfully and wonderfully made. You are an overcomer in Christ Jesus. You are the righteousness of God in Christ. You are more than a conqueror in Christ. You are victorious in every area of your life. You are the head and not the tail. You are restored, delivered, whole, nothing missing, nothing broken. You live in abundance and have no lack. God meets all your needs according to his riches in glory in Christ Jesus. You are the healed. Jesus took all your sickness and carried all your disease.

    A believer fights the battles that come FROM victory. We do not fight to obtain but we have already obtained when we received Jesus as Lord and Savior and the enemy is trying to take what is ours. The enemy will do all he can to get your focus off God and his word and promises and finished work of Jesus. Don't fall into unbelief. Having done all to stand, stand with your armor on. Read *Ephesians 6:10-20.*

Chapter Six

Relationships

Another big factor in relationships is being there for those you profess to love. True love will not intentionally harm you and will consider your needs before their own needs. They will always think "Is this going to help our relationship or will this harm it and tear down what we have been working on building?" There is only one response in love. Love will not do anything that may harm, tear down or destroy what it loves. Love will always be there considering the loved even if that means personal sacrifice on their part. Even our children, when they have gone against what you knew was best for them and they got themselves in trouble, a person of real love would still be there to encourage and teach them through their tough time, even though it is an inconvenience to them and that they have to put their wants and desires on hold in order to show your love, guidance, encouragement and support that things will get better. It's quite a sacrifice at times to do well by another and to show love to another.

Simple Steps To A Better Life

Relationships are the biggest part in your life that the world will still at least acknowledge. We have many different kinds of relationships. We have business relationships, acquaintance relationships, and friend and family relationships. We have an extra special relationship (hopefully) with our parents and with our spouse. These two relationships are even closer and then our number one closest relationship should always be with God. After all He already knows all about us, there is no reason to lie to the one who knows everything. It would kind of be like you, trying to lie to you. That would be a stupid thing to do but let me tell you there are plenty of people who lie to themselves every day and they have lied for so long to themselves, that now they believe their lies. What a major deception! Lying in relationships will always destroy the relationship and it will also prevent growth in that relationship.

Really I would like to focus on positives, or things you should do rather than things that you shouldn't. Love, care, concern and understanding are all things that will add to any relationship. Trust is another big factor in relationships and growth. These qualities present in any relationship will cause the relationship to flourish. Growth is eminent if given the right ingredients.

Time spent with the other you are trying to grow in relationship with is always helpful. You must be sure not to try to dominate the relationship. Don't always think that you have to have your own way. Remember that when you met, you just wanted to know all about them and do the things that they did, to share your life with them. You were more than happy that the other person wanted to and chose to share their life with you. Then suddenly it seems that somewhere down the road you decided that getting the "leftovers" of time was not enough. You want to have the rule of their life; you get a wrong mindset that they should no longer do the things that they used to enjoy because it takes time away from you. This is unfortunately a common outlook for people who have no experience in having good relationships. There are actually quite a few people that I know, that think once they get married that they are going to change things about their spouse. This is a huge deception. Yes, people change but not at the spouses command. I always tell the boys look closely and be very picky because what you see you better be sure you can handle it because there is no guarantee that it will ever change to the way you think it should be or to what you want and once you are married it is for life.

Don't fool yourself; never go into a relationship thinking that you will ever be able to change anyone and don't think that trying to dominate them and make them do what you want is going to work out either. Eventually the dominated one will wake up and run for all it's worth, to try and find themselves and learn to be their own person again.

You can either both accept a person's flaws and live with them or you can't and won't, but this is something that only you with Gods guidance can answer. Unless God tells you something on the matter there is no other person on this earth that knows you well enough to contribute to making that decision for you. If we are really honest, it is a decision that only God knows the answer to. We may put up with something one day and decide that we don't want to take it anymore the next. Only God truly knows what is best for you.

Relationships require a lot of work. You can't ignore them and think it will all work out. If at all possible, you must keep open lines of communication. You must talk and you must listen and you need to be understanding of their views and opinions, also you should be accepting of their view and/or opinion, even if you don't see it or if it is different from yours.

People are entitled to choose and see things the way they choose, whether we agree or not you must respect their right to make that choice, no matter how painful it may be to you. That is our God given right and we must accept that right and give it to all people. Everyone receives their own rewards or consequences for their own choices and we have to give them that right.

A relationship is not a one sided thing. It takes two to make it work and it takes two to break it. Although you cannot force someone to stay in relationship with you, you can keep the lines open and friendly, yet still give them their space to figure themselves out. If your spouse chooses to leave you then you have to love them enough to let them go. You cannot force anyone to stay with you and you shouldn't want to. If you truly love them, you want them to be happy whether that is with you or not, because true love will put another's happiness before their own. Just do yourself a favor and see what things you could have done differently and learn from your mistakes so you are not repeating your flaws that contributed to the relationships dissolution.

We must be careful who we allow ourselves to be in relationship with. Coming into relationship always means opening yourself up to it and we should always watch that it is a mutual relationship. Some people don't really care and they can hurt you very badly if you choose to ignore the signs.

Are you both equally putting into this relationship?

Is the other stand off-ish?

Do they allow you in, as much as you allow them in?

Or are they reserved?

You can't have one who gives but never takes, nor can you have one who takes and never gives. There must be a balance so we are able to help the other refuel throughout life.

Now I will tell you again, God knows the person that He made for you, to be with you through it all. Are you going to follow His leading or are you going to rush out and do it on your own, thinking that you know better than God. I will tell you this, if you know in your heart that you are in a relationship that God hasn't chosen for you, but yet you persist to continue in it, or maybe even marry it, you will have a hard time being happy and it may work into more distressing situations in the future.

Any time that you intentionally go against Gods will, you have made the choice to make your life harder than it needs to be, until you repent (change your mind), and start following Gods leading again.

We need to learn to do things in faith, with a clear conscience, believing that this is what we believe God wants us to do. Don't ever think that you can go against God and that it will work out well. If you go against Him intentionally then you had better also be preparing yourself to suffer the consequences of your actions.

God says not to be unevenly yoked and this is an important thing to remember. You want someone that shares the same faith and moral fiber as you so that the two of you will agree wholeheartedly as to the path you will follow to reach the goal you have set.

If you are unevenly yoked you will have so many struggles as to acceptable behaviors and actions along the way, that at times life may seem unbearable. That is not to say you can't bear it, I am sure you can with God's help, but it is allowing for many more "bumps" in the road than would be if you were evenly yoked with the same beliefs and morals.

The compromises that you may make in your own character and integrity through this may not be something you will want to live with down the road and may also open the door for bitterness and resentment down the road. You don't want to open yourself to attacks of this nature. This is why it is better not to be unevenly yoked together, whether it is a marriage or a business transaction, weigh all life decisions carefully.

Your thought should be to keep yourself pure and think on things that are pure good, lovely and of good report on matters. You will soon be living in the thoughts you have chosen to believe, so why would you want to think on anything less than something that will give you good results and a good heritage.

One of the hardest things you need to do to keep good relationships is to not fight or allow strife in. You may find it very hard to continue in love and kindness when what you are receiving from the person is bitterness and hatred, but with Gods help and perspective you will be able to.

The way God has shown me, I am to love the person regardless and realize that they are deceived in their thinking. That is what makes them act the way they do and given to lack of self-control. I am to pray for them and forgive them, knowing that God has allowed us to be in this position for good, so we can be a witness of Gods goodness flowing out of us to them. I will tell you outright; if you have any pride or self-righteousness you will not be able to do this. If, through practice and leaning on God you continue doing good regardless, you will overcome and eventually it will become easier and easier.

Using this "kill them with love and kindness" method will not only help you to die to self but it may also save marriages and bring newness to relationships that are in need of TLC (tender loving care).

I believe that if someone wants to leave you and you treat them the absolute best you can, giving extra attention, kindness and love, and with Holy Spirit, their minds can be changed and they will not want to let go of all the goodness and encouragement you have been pouring out to them. That is the recipe for saving a marriage. It takes a courageous and confident person and that's exactly who we are in Christ. Nothing is impossible to the believer in Christ.

Being kind and loving to those who don't deserve it will make you more like Jesus. After all, isn't that what he did for us? And we are called to do the same. When you have mastered this you will have good relationships and be that much closer to joy unspeakable and heaven on earth.

Chapter Seven

Motives

God knows your heart and He knows your every motive. He knows you better than you know yourself and if you watch your actions He will reveal to you your motives if you truly want to know. God will help you with all your endeavors. No matter what you are attempting to do, according to the word of God with regard to your request of Him, He will prosper everything you put your hand to. As long as you choose what is right according to His word and you acknowledge Him in all your ways with a clean heart and pure motives there is no way you will ever fail.

Your motives are what your actions will be judged against. Your motive is the reason why you do something. Ask yourself "why do I want to do this?" Is it to hurt someone who hurt me? Is it a payback for an offense cause to me by this person? If you say yes or if you know that it will cause harm then there is no way you should convince yourself that you are doing it with a good motive. If you succeed you will cause deception in your life and that will open up a whole other world of problems for you.

Your motives should always be with good intent, to do another good and not harm. Yes wrong things happen to us and others appear to be getting away with their wrong motivated actions, but this is not us or who we are in Christ.

We are children of the light and we chose repeatedly to walk in whatever light we have in order to grow in the grace of God. We chose to show mercy and forgive as God has shown mercy on us and forgiven us.

We will not fall into the traps set to keep us from the glory of God. God says that as we sow, so shall we reap. If we chose to want to live in Gods best then we must walk in His best even when it is hard and especially when it is undesirable to do so. If we cannot be trusted to keep our feelings under submission to God then how can we keep the other areas of life that we have little control over in submission?

God blessed you with feelings and sin came and perverted those feelings. We live in a "if it feels good do it" society. This is the worst deception of all. Feelings change constantly. You cannot count on them. The way you feel about something is your choice and unfortunately, this is not taught this way anymore. No one can make you feel a certain way. Either you chose to look at it one way, with understanding and refusal to take offense, which will cause you to feel good about yourself, or, you will allow yourself to be offended and take personally the situation and then you will have bad feelings about others and yourself.

Simple Steps To A Better Life

You must choose not to take things personally or you will always be upset with someone. Then when you are upset it causes stress and stress causes chemical imbalances, which can lead to cancer and low self-worth and a whole host of other things. If you choose to continue to hang on to things, then years later you will see that you have become a bitter person and the worst part is because you wouldn't forgive the other, you have shut the door for God to forgive you. I pray that you will not choose to keep this kind of misery in your life. You can't always be upset with people and enjoy your life at the same time. You will wind up doing things in an attempt to dull or numb the pain that you have chosen not let go of.

On the other hand, if you let go of the hurt another has caused you then you have given God a place to work in both of your lives. The moment that you pray for the offender and ask God to bless them, despite the fact that every fiber in your body is against it, but you have made a choice and mustered the resolve to carry it out, then know this, the first thing that God is going to bless them with is the knowledge of the hurt they have caused.

I find it enlightening to know that by my doing what's right in this situation, I have not only opened a door for God to bless me and give me "double for my trouble", but I have also opened the door for God to save that person from a life separated from God. That alone is the best reason to forgive and pray for those who do you wrong, for their salvation.

It is funny how some people will pray for their offender. They pray they have a slow painful death or try to pray some curse on them. Let me tell you, if this sounds like your prayer then you defiantly have wrong motives. You definitely are not showing that you want to do them good all the days of your life. I would recommend that if this is your prayer, pray for crop failure and repent immediately and ask God to give you a clean heart, I am sure that praying prayers of this nature have you in a place of self-infliction. Get out quick!

James 3 **(Heavenly Versus Demonic Wisdom)**
13 Who *is* wise and understanding among you? Let him show by good conduct *that* his works *are done* in the meekness of wisdom. 14 But if you have bitter envy and self-seeking in your hearts, do not boast and lie against the truth. 15 This wisdom does not descend from above, but *is* earthly, sensual, demonic. 16 For where envy and self-seeking *exist,* confusion and every evil thing *are* there. 17 But the wisdom that is from above is first pure, then peaceable, gentle, willing to yield, full of mercy and good fruits, without partiality and without hypocrisy. 18 Now the fruit of righteousness is sown in peace by those who make peace. (NKJV)

Simple Steps To A Better Life

You cannot fool God. He knows your motives for the things you do, even when you don't. Be sure your motives are ones that will truly show Gods character within you and you will find that you look at yourself differently and feel better about yourself for being a nicer person. You will find you no longer want to get even with people, that you pray for them and their salvation out of a pure heart and concern for the path and choices they have put themselves in. You will become a more loving and peaceful person.

There may come times when you need to stay clear from people (even family) because they are on a path that you cannot condone. You see the pain they inflict on themselves and everyone around them and you have to sometimes make the decision to "steer clear" of them. For two reasons: first, because you don't want to give them the impression that you are accepting of their wrong actions, and secondly, for your own self-preservation. There are times that I just want certain people to stay away from my loved ones and me. I don't want to deal with all the drama they have produced in their life, the pain they have tried to put on people that they laugh about. I don't want to hear it. I don't think it's funny and I think that their brain and their thinking are off kilter. Usually I only tell them "I'm not accepting house guests at this time" after I have tried to talk with them and they just don't care what they are doing to the people around them because they are so selfish they can't see past themselves and will gladly tear apart and make miserable anyone they can.

    I don't want my kids to think this is acceptable behavior, and I really don't want to have to deal with all the junk that is stirred up for the time they are here. God says we are to protect ourselves, or we may fall into their "sin" with them while we are trying to help them out. If someone becomes intrusive on your life don't feel bad to tell them, "This is not a good time" and send them on their way. Sometimes it makes all the difference in the preservation of your own life.

    It is unfortunate that some people do not see or want help to live a better life in Christ. We cannot force them. God gave them free will and if they are not interested in changing their life for the better you do not need to keep them front and center in your life. I would still pray for them. God wishes that none would perish and that all should come to repentance.

    Always remember that the reason why you do something is very important and will be revealed by God and you will be rewarded accordingly. Whatever we do should all be done for good and as unto the Lord and for the glory of God.

Chapter Eight
Preparation for the Purpose

    The only people who ever fail are the ones who give up. As long as you persist and refuse to be overcome, as long as you stand you will eventually overcome. One of my favorite sayings is "This too will pass, Things will not remain the same" and really, it is the truth.

    Life is a series of changes. Nothing is ever the same in this world. The only thing that never changes is God. He is and will be the same yesterday, today and forever. His word will not pass away although everything else as we know it will pass away. God won't, nor will his word. He is the only thing in this life that is stable. He is the only thing that will last forever.

    I pray that each of you who read this will one day, very shortly, come to know the magnitude and the awesomeness of His presence, if you don't already know it. Some things cannot be explained. Some things you can never learn or know until you experience it for yourself. A completely whole, fulfilling and loving relationship cannot be phantom without believing, seeking and experiencing it for yourself. There is nothing like your own experiences to help you to relate to another. Sometimes I think that God allows me to go through things so that I am able to relate to others and help them through something similar that they find difficult.

I don't really believe that all I go through is for me alone. I believe it is all part of a higher plan. As it was for Joseph, all he had to go through so he would wind up at the right place at the right time in God's divine will for him. Without him being in the position he was in, many would have died from famine. The food would not have been put aside to make it through those years of famine. Yes, Joseph had to go through it but it wasn't solely for him, it was so he would have the proper character and integrity to assume the position God had for him.

God also has a position for you. It may not be the same as what you think, but none the less, each of us was created for a purpose. Your importance is in God's plan. This purpose will never be found without God. We need to go through things in order to grow and understand others and the place they are at. It is impossible to help someone through a situation when you don't have a clue and can't relate. We are here to overcome and then help others overcome as well.

The pieces of the picture that we see are tiny in comparison to the whole scheme of things in God's plan. Don't be hasty and think wrongly when you go through things. For everything that happens God has chosen to use us according to His purpose.

When my son at age 3 wound up having leukemia, it was extremely hard for me to see Gods plan, but against all I was told and I saw, I knew God had a use for this in His plan and that no matter what happened, He was in control. I found scriptures and stood on them. I would have my son speak them, my vigor caused him to come to life and say it like he believed it. This was a time I could not be mousy "well Lord if it be your will", none of that came from this family. This was a matter of life and death and the bible clearly states that "Jesus bore all our sickness and carried our disease and by His stripes you were healed", well if we were, then we are and the thief is trying to steal from you again! Well you better not sit back and take it, unless you are ready to go home, you better stand on your promises!

We have a blood covenant with God and He clearly lists all you are entitled to in the covenant with Him. If you chose to let someone steal from you then I am sure they will. Otherwise you better get your words in line with the promises you have and get your faith going and prepare for a battle. You need to decide to live as God tells you in His word you can, let nothing sway you from the truth, especially your feelings and of course your mind and thoughts will have to be watched carefully and kept in line.

Simple Steps To A Better Life

Your motives must be watched, so as not to become selfish, like "God save my husband so he will be nicer to me" or "Heal my son so I don't have to go through this pain".

Five years this family went through circumstances trying to tear us apart. Our first son, Jonathan, was 7 years old when Michael (age 3) was diagnosed, we just had our third child, Henry Jr. (7 months old) and we lived a couple hours from the hospital. I stayed with Michael in the hospital; my husband kept working up north, to support the family. Jonathan, (7 at the time) would come home from school and cook dinner for dad. My grandmother, Alice, kept the baby, Henry Jr. with her; she was 45 minutes from the hospital. Henry Sr. would come every night he could after work, to stay with Mike while I went to see Nana Alice and the baby. This went on for years, with hospital stays sometimes consuming a month at a time.

I'm telling you this so you can see that things are tough at times, but with God there is nothing that can't be overcome. Michael is 29 now and he has been in remission since the first week of treatment. So much time has passed that even the doctors call him healed, but we had the faith to believe God and knew he was healed from the beginning. Sometimes things happen in our lives that we have no control over and through those moments I believe that if God has allowed it, then He intends on using it and it must be part of His higher plan. I consider the things I have gone through in my life to be part of the preparation for the purpose God has for me. I acknowledge that all the things I have gone through have made me the person that I am. I know through my relationship with God that He is in control of all things concerning me and I have enough faith in Him to know that He knows what is best for me, knowing that, I would never want to change what I have gone through. I consider it all preparation for the purpose He has called me to.

Although you may be in a place where it seems that things are falling apart, don't go with your feelings. Change your feelings to line up with the word. God knows every choice you have made and are going to make. All things are naked and open to Him. There is nothing He doesn't know and nothing He hasn't worked into His plan. God is never surprised. I believe that everything is in preparation for the purpose He has for us.

During this time we are learning of God and growing in knowledge of His word and His character. We are developing a relationship. The more time we spend in the Word learning and talking with God the deeper and more intimate our relationship becomes. Through our experiences we learn to lean, trust and rely on him in and through all things.

We are King's kids and there are many things that we need to learn regarding Kingdom life. We are to know the Kingdom principles and put them into practice here and now that "Thy kingdom come, thy will be done on earth as it is in Heaven" we should see manifesting in every area of our life. We need to know the kingdom principles before we can live by them and bring them into manifestation in our lives. We must hear before we can believe and only then can we know.

Father, we thank you for the Word and Holy Spirit. We thank you for revelation knowledge. Teach us as only you can. Let us continually be prepared for your purpose. Help us to know you in a deeper and more intimate way than ever before. We thank you and praise you for your mighty work in our lives. Let me be an empty vessel (empty of myself) fit for the your use. Thank you that we are blessed and all we put our hand to prospers. Thank you for making our paths straight.

Chapter Nine
Compromise - The Character Killer

There are many things in life that we don't understand. That is because we don't see the big picture. We only see a small piece of the puzzle. Only through God's revelation can we ever get the vantage point of Gods'. Truly you will never even be able to comprehend Gods plan without first renewing your mind.

There is only one way to renew your mind and that is to read and believe the word of God even when sometimes what your reading is unbelievable, you will have to make the clear concise choice to believe it, regardless how much it doesn't go along with everything you have been taught throughout your life or the way you perceive your life at this moment. We, people in general and especially parents do what we perceive to be the best for those we have influence over. We generally give our best for the circumstances we are in and to the best of our ability and our knowledge. There are very few parents who intentionally and with clear motive hurt, misinform, and lead our loved ones astray. But yet at times, through the compromise we have allowed in our own lives, we wind up passing those compromises down to our children, friends and families, without intention of harm or knowledge of the same.

Compromise is when you know what is right to do, but you allow and make exception for it, usually thinking that this one small minute detail is not going to make that big of a difference. Let me tell you, every decision you decide to make against your better judgment is a place in your personality and life that you have allowed compromise to creep in and each of those seemingly small areas when contributed to repeatedly become very large areas and character flaws.

Compromise of what you know is the right thing to do, will slowly but surely, (if not repented of and turned from) destroy your character and integrity. What seemingly is a very small thing, that you would not think would have a great impact on your life and that would have no strength to grow and become a powerful force in your life, will do just that, if allowed. Just as one lie will lead to another and another to cover the last, then before you know it it's out of control and you are surprised how large the one little lie has become through time and covering. This same thing is true in all areas, if you chose to disregard what you know is the right thing then each time you make that choice your conscience becomes quieter and quieter in that area until you hear it say nothing to you about it anymore. It is almost like you give up on yourself. Ultimately you still know it's wrong but there is no inward resistance (conscience) to help you to make the right and better choice anymore. You have worn it down through your continuance to disregard your spirit (conscience) and make the wrong choices. You have opened yourself to a self-created deception. You now believe, that the wrong you do is ok, because your conscience no longer strives against the wrong. This wrong has now become acceptable behavior to yourself and you have convinced yourself that it is ok. You have justified your wrong choice for so long, that you think it is acceptable through your own justification. Although this wrong, depending on its nature, may not take you to hell, it will bring you a judgment for the actions. It will be something to be answered for if not overcome and repented for previously in this life before you are no longer in this world. It will keep you from the fullness that God has set aside for you, because in that area you cannot be trusted, you have not come to maturity in that area. There are rewards and benefit to each level of maturity and responsibility and you will never know all that you are missing until you overcome and live in the blessings that come with the new level.

    I am not saying that there should be no compromise in your life at all. What I am saying is that when it comes to God, His word and His ways, compromise should never be an option. Now there are many other things that we will come to in life, that compromise must be taken advantage of and used. This is usually taken advantage of in the form of "peacemaker" type issues and will never be something that is against God and His ways, but it is used to keep peace, show genuine care and usually always is utilized in relation to tastes and opinions of our own. You may compromise on the kind, color or style of a home or vehicle. You may compromise when it comes to your own wants and desires to make another happy. This type of compromise can also be more in the line of sacrifice. Perhaps parents go without things they desire in order to fulfill their child's life the best they can or maybe they make sacrifices in order to help their children through a rough patch in their life even though their rough patch was caused through their own rebellion and refusing to honor their parents' instruction. True love will always seek the best for the loved person. Love will not seek its own but will seek after the best for the other. Love does not harm or intentionally hurt another. Love will not require its own ways. Love is very unique, it is all things to all people and all people require it in order to have a fulfilled and happy life. Everyone seems to have a different piece of love and everyone's understanding of love is at different levels. None of us, myself included, have the fullness and wholeness of love mastered and we never will, until we meet our maker and He transforms us into the image of His son Jesus, who is the example of all that is love, for God is love and love is God. Without God existing in your life you would not know what love is because if love is there then God is there. The two cannot be separated; they are one in the same.

    We never compromise when it comes to doing what is right. We however will compromise our desire, in order to help fulfill another's life and this sacrifice that we make is love. This is only one part of love. Love has many facets and is something that in your whole life you will never know the true depth and fullness of. We must always be striving though to know more and come to a greater fullness of Love. Love is the ultimate goal and to know love is to know God. When you experience love you are experiencing God. Without God is to be without love. They are inseparable. When you realize this you will be able to better see His work in your life, but understand there are many who have a twisted or perverted sense of love and you should never mistake human love as the guide line. God and His love is the only true measuring stick and no other type of love should be thought to be the truest or purest form. God's love is the only true and pure love; all others are a lesser and lower level of love. The only way to experience pure and true love in its greatest form available is to know Jesus and the love God and He have for you, only then will you be able to know the purest form of love available on this earth.

God wants to have a relationship with you, that is His ultimate desire. Your part is to choose to have the relationship and to make it first and foremost in your life. As you walk with Him, He will give you knowledge and wisdom (how to use the knowledge). As you move forward without compromise of the knowledge you have learned from Him, you will grow in character and integrity. As you show yourself faithful you will also be putting yourself in position to receive more and more from Him. Sometimes it seems as though we grow through trials, and believe me trials will come. I always keep in mind that if I wasn't a threat to Satan then I wouldn't be attacked and my family wouldn't be attacked the way we are. I know that we are headed for something better and God is allowing us to make the decisions that we do, in order to get us where we need to be so He can advance us to the next level and give us greater responsibility and privilege. Generally, we have to go through some things first. So, don't get weary in doing what is right and don't compromise when it comes to God and His ways and you will come out in the end, in a place more successful then you could have ever believed. You can reach the goal and live in the high calling of knowing God and ultimately be a complete success as long as you don't give up, cave in and quit.

    Don't compromise when it comes to God and what He has made you for. Always do your best, to be your best. Do the right thing and let God do the rest, you can trust Him. He will give you a fulfilling and love filled life.

Chapter Ten
Rebellion brings Deception

There is no person who is perfect and without flaw walking this earth at the present time. We all are human and we all have made mistakes. Although you occasionally run into those who are very pious and esteem themselves higher than all others and do their best to make you believe they are without flaw and are perfect. Those who know Gods word, know that this is an outright deception and that this seemingly innocent deception will carry over to many areas in one's life. That one thought will breed a wrong attitude in many areas, how you think about others, wrong thoughts about yourself and your worth.

All sin that was brought into this world was brought here through one wrong thought. Satan had a wrong thought about himself. He thought he was as good as his Creator. Through this one wrong thought came a wrong attitude about himself and his purpose the creator had for him. Through his refusal to bring that wrong thought captive at the onset, he began meditating and believing the deception until he believed the deception to be the truth. This is how rebellion started and continued to grow and still grows in individuals.

Selfishness also will breed rebellion. The "what about me?", "What's in it for me?" attitude will cause you to do things you know are not the "right thing" to do. You will deceive yourself into a place where you believe that "its o.k. because by doing this, it will better my life in some way". Let me tell you, thinking only of yourself and the benefit that you may get from the wrong, will never "better your life". The end result of doing wrong things will always bring bad things, bad consequences in the end, bitter conscience and bad thoughts of yourself (labeled today as low self-esteem, alcoholism, drug abuse, etc.) This is why it is so important to know who you are in Christ, but you will not ever come to know that when you are in rebellion. Rebellion will always cause you to miss the mark.

Rebellion will always cause deception. If you are living in rebellion, then it is obvious that you don't know who you are. If you are living in rebellion, then you have already accepted wrong thinking and have separated yourself from Him. He is always there waiting for you to turn, but you have pulled away and chosen to believe the lie. That is where rebellion comes from. If you know better but aren't doing better then you need to check your thinking. Somewhere in there is a thought, that is a lie and you have chosen to believe the lie. I am sure that you have justified the thought in order for you to accept it.

Simple Steps To A Better Life

The only way to clean out your mind is to pray to God to reveal it to you through His word and then to read His word until the bad thought is gone and the change in your actions is accomplished. You will realize that Gods word has again been given precedence. You will realize that your perspective is different and your attitude has changed. This is what is needed to overcome wrong thoughts and rebellion.

You will find that with God, His ways are simple. There is no complicated or elaborate plan. His plan and ways are simple. Simple does not mean easy. Simple yes, if the solution isn't simple then it has probably been complicated by man and religion. Easy, that is another story. Usually although it is simple, it is not an easy thing to do. It usually takes hard work, determination and discipline to accomplish this "simple" thing.

We must always watch ourselves and when we see that we are in rebellion in an area, (or don't agree with the word of God) that we have allowed in deceptive thinking, we must ask God to help us with our rebellion and get back in the word and agree with the word over what we think or feel.

Regardless of what we think or feel we must make a clear concise choice to believe the word over all else. This is the only way that we can overcome rebellion. We must take every thought captive and bring each thought under the authority of God and into agreement with His word.

We cannot think that if we rebel against God, that we will not fall into deception of some sort. We must realize the power that we give to the thoughts we meditate on. We will hurt ourselves if we refuse to bring our thoughts into agreement with God's word. Meditating on wrong thoughts, will lead to wrong actions and wrong actions, will bring unpleasant consequences.

Refuse to walk in rebellion and keep yourself from the deception that will follow.

Father, I thank you that your anointing is able to destroy every yoke. Have your way in my life. I choose to believe your word. I bring every thought captive into the obedience of Christ.

Read *2 Corinthians 10:3-6*

Chapter Eleven
Believing vs. Trying

    You can only grow to the extent you believe in all things. Whether good or bad beliefs, you will accomplish and live out what you believe. That is why I am always telling my children "Your life is only what you make of it. Your life is in your hands to excel and succeed or to lie down and be defeated, you have complete control." God has given you a manual to instruct you on proper use of this gift of life.

    Many of us dig into this life without reading the instruction manual and many times when things go wrong, many still won't go to the manual and follow the instructions. This is to our own demise. You will never know all the features and benefits of this life until you read, learn and understand all the instructions provided in the bible.

    Many choose not to go all the way. They just get enough to get by and have use for the very basic purpose and never go any further. Maybe because they feel they "tried" and it didn't work. You will never accomplish anything with that attitude.

Simple Steps To A Better Life

People who "try" are defeated on every turn. They give up easily and have no faith or stamina.

Anything in life worth having is going to take effort. Anyone who is consistent and determined will not be denied. They will have what they are standing for even if it takes 20 years, and for some things you are waiting for, it might take that long. You see a true Christian never gives up, caves in or quits. They will not try, they will push and believe and stand until they see the manifestation they are looking for. They have found their scripture and are going to believe and stand on it, until it has manifested itself. They will succeed and will not except failure. They will continue to press toward the mark for the prize of the high calling. That prize is to know Him, in all His fullness and power. You will never get to know Him by simply "trying". You must believe, move forward and receive.

If you're trying, you don't believe. The two work against each other. Someone who tries doesn't believe. Someone who believes doesn't try. The two are opposite lifestyles. The believer does and keeps doing until victory is accomplished. Someone who tries only does so until resistance comes and then quits and says "I tried and it didn't work". This is a phrase you will never hear from a true believer. A believer knows, that he knows, that he knows, that through patient endurance it will be accomplished. Their will is in line with Gods will and their heart carries the desires of Gods heart. They will stand, push and do all they can until the victory has manifested in their life. Believers do and do and do some more until they have done all they can do, then they still don't give up. They stand and wait for God to bring it to pass and when the opportunity arises again, they do more toward reaching the goal. Their battle is not with flesh and blood but with principalities and powers and the ruler of the darkness of this world. They do not war with earthen vessels (other people) the war is in the spiritual realm. They do not back down or accept defeat, nor do they doubt God's word. There is no question as to whether God's word will work or not. They know that God's word is true and that anyone who speaks against it does not know God.

    Our battle is within ourselves, in our mind and thinking. We believe the word of God and work with Holy Spirit to keep the truth of Gods word rooted in our heart and running the thoughts and attitudes of our person. We continually guard our heart and mind by watching every thought and meditation that they are in line with Gods word. We keep our thoughts on the good, pure, lovely, good report, in praise, worship and thanksgiving to God. *(Philippians 4:8)* Any thought that does not line up with Gods word and is not good, we bring it into captivity and change or replace it to agree with the word and what God says we are to think on and the way He shows us through the word to form our perceptions. *(2 Corinthians 10:5)*

    The word gives us hope and causes faith to rise in us so we are able to accomplish all that God has set before us. This is why it is important to be in the word, to let it fill your mind and heart and meditate on it. The word gives us gifts of knowledge and brings us into a closer, deeper and more personal relationship with God in Christ. Through our believing with our whole heart, we gain understanding and God is permitted access to accomplish within us what needs to be done to bring us to maturity in our soul area. Once the soul has prospered it will overflow into the natural world (the seen) in that area. *(3 John 1:2)*

Believers know the goal will be met and success is assured, Jesus finished the work and gave us the victory, it's all just a matter of time and faith and believers trusting God so much that they are able to enter into the peace and rest of God. God never fails and He will accomplish all he has set out to.

Believers will hope, lean, trust and rely on God especially when it looks like there is no hope in the natural (seen) world. They will fight to stay in Gods peace and rest. It is in that rest that we are able to stay lined up with and living in the kingdom principles. All this can only be obtained and experienced through making the conscious choice to believe God and his word above all else. Believing is our one required action.

Chapter Twelve

Everyone makes mistakes

God has made provision for all our mess-ups. For every mistake, He made a plan, a path if you will, to bring His outcome. Our God knows all things. He knows us better than we know ourselves. He knows our choices before we even know there will be a decision we will have to make. He has already compensated for the wrong decisions He knows that we are going to make. He knows the end from the beginning. You need not get worried that you have made a mistake and that God can't help you. God already knew the choices you would make and He built in a way out for you, as long as you repent and make Him Lord of your life, He will forgive you and show you the plan He still holds for you. He made provision for you, regardless of mistakes, for you to overcome and fulfill His plan for you.

We must always move forward and do our best to do what is right. We must have mercy and forgiveness for those who have done wrong just as God gives us mercy and forgiveness for our wrong doings. We are not to esteem ourselves higher than we ought to. We want to steer clear from pride and "looking down" on others. We must always remember "if not for the grace of God, there go I" when we are viewing others. We are in sin when we place ourselves above others. We are all God's children and he loves us all the same. His love never changes and it is the same for all of us. He loves the preacher who saves thousands just the same as the housewife who consistently does what's right. It doesn't stop there; He loves the sinner who rejects Him just as much as the prior two. We are all created equal and loved by God just as much as the next person. We have to be sure that we do not look down on others for any reason. If you do, whether you realize it or not, you are judging them and opening yourself up for judgment upon yourself. God says, with what measure you use toward others, God will measure you with that same measurement. So for your own sake, don't judge others or be cruel to them, because what you give out in this life, it will be given back to you. Be sure to take the time and look at yourself and treat others as you want to be treated. Don't hand out something to another that you wouldn't want handed to you. Do to others as you would want done to you. This is a great principle to live by.

There is no one who is so perfect in this world that can make it to heaven without the blood of Jesus. Do not deceive yourself thinking you are above another of Gods children in stature, you are not. We are all equal in His sight and He says, for all have sinned and fallen short of the glory of God. Be forgiving and know that we all make mistakes.

Chapter Thirteen
Judge Yourself, Not Others

    Without a doubt, we will be judged according to our motives and our choices and with the same standard of judgment that we use to measure others. That is why it's best not to judge others, just be as understanding as possible and do your best not to have negative opinions of others and their choices. I am not saying withhold correction, but do not think lowly of them because of the error of their ways.

    Always remember, most people value suggestions, almost everyone doesn't really want your opinion. There is a difference and you need to know that difference. Suggestions are usually given and taken in a caring, helpful manner, as is correction. Opinions tend to be given and received as harsh and judgmental. Many times, there is not a problem with the point you are trying to make, it is the way you serve it, that is rejected. Opinions tend to shut people down and put them on defense. Suggestions tend to open people up to further conversations. Presentation is everything and you need to learn to present yourself properly if you want to help someone and receive a positive response.

Simple Steps To A Better Life

We may see what others do, but we never know their motives that determine their choices. Only God knows the motives and intent of another, unless that person has clearly stated or shown their motives. Even when another tells us their motive, it is very unlikely that we will understand fully, unless they tell us the whole and both sides are heard. We cannot make an honest and true judgment with only a piece of information. We do not see fully all things that have determined their decision. We are not called to judge others. We are called to judge ourselves. We need to take off the mask and look at the true person in the mirror. We need to stop making excuses for ourselves and our actions. We need to stop blaming others for "the way we are". As long as you continue to lay blame on others, then you have justified it within yourself and you are doing yourself a great disservice because you will never change your problem. Yes, that's right, it is YOUR problem, not your mother, not your father, not your spouse, not your children's, it is YOUR problem, and you will continue to be miserable and make others miserable until YOU stop blaming the rest of the world for your problems. At some point you are going to have to grow up and take responsibility for your life.

Your life is a product of the way you chose to view your life, choices you chose to make. Yes, I know bad things happen to us, when we were little we didn't have good parents, maybe some of us didn't have any parents but that is still no excuse. You choose whether to allow your circumstances to hold you back or

Simple Steps To A Better Life

to refuse those negative beginnings and press on and make a better life and be a better person despite your past and things you have gone through. You will never be able to better your life while you are blaming others for it.

Take responsibility for yourself and your actions. Stop going around blaming your parents and your spouse for all your misfortune. Grow up and get a grip on your life. Forgive and let go of all the things you have been holding against people for years. Then and only then will you realize that your life and the circumstances within it were what YOU chose, and how you chose to view those instances shaped your thinking, but now that you aren't hiding and justifying your actions you will be able to change your thoughts, perceptions and your circumstances and it will change your life.

You will never get anywhere playing the blame game. You will just continue circling around that mountain again and again, and you will continually keep getting the same results, the same heartache, and the same pain. Unfortunately, it is because you continue to choose it over and over. You keep doing the same things expecting different results. That is insanity! If you want a change, make a change, and start with YOU! Change yourself, not your parents, boss, friends, spouse or children – change yourself.

I feel bad for the people that hear a good message or are given good advice but they refuse to take it for themselves. It is," oh, I hope my wife was listening because they were preaching for her", or for someone else, always pointing out the flaws of another, when they should be taking the message and applying it against their own life. They are in such deception that they don't even realize they are in worse shape than the person that they want to give the sermon to! The people that do this will not change because they are still thinking it is everyone else in the world that has to change to make them happy. They take no responsibility for themselves or their life. It is always about what everyone else did to them and they play themselves off as the innocent one who just "is stuck with whatever they are dished".

    As long as people continue to blame others for their misfortune, they will never change or help bring their selves into a better life. The life God has set aside for them, again it is their choice to make the change or not. No one can get through or make them see it until they are ready, so unfortunately the most you can do is be brutally honest when they ask you what you think the problem is or what you would do. You can make suggestions and guide them, give them scripture to meditate on, but until they want to see it, they won't.

    If you continue correcting an adult, that really doesn't want to do all they can do to correct their problem, you will find it becomes draining. There have been times that I have repeated the same thing over and over for long periods of time and still the person refused the truth and basically just kept calling to hash the same thing over and over, without ever doing anything to make a change that would improve their situation, they basically continued to inflict more and more pain not only on themselves but on all the people that were close to them. At times, I wish I had tape recorded our conversation so I could just play it for them as much as they needed to hear it, because when they called, honestly, I was tired of repeating myself for the past year, and I know that until they take responsibility, nothing would change. It was always the same thing over and over. I don't know what they thought, that on a day to day basis they had to call to test me to see if my response would change? Well, the bible didn't change so why would my response? But even through all this, I did my best not to be judgmental and to state the options available and the responses or consequences that may follow depending on the optional choice they made. I would remind them that it was their choices that sent them further into misfortune, but they would not take responsibility; in their mind it is everyone else's fault. All that can be done in this situation is pray that their eyes be opened to see the truth. When you are drained just let them know "This is not a good time" and steer clear if you need to. You don't want this to become a gossip session. You don't want to drain yourself down so far that you are starting to feel consumed, burdened and oppressed by the situation. You will be hard pressed to help someone up and out when you aren't able to keep your peace and proper perspective. Remember the enemy is always trying to distract you from the truth of the word so you won't use it and come out victorious.

Until they take responsibility for their lives, and determine that they want a change, they won't make a change. All we can do is pray, pray, and pray against this stronghold in their mind. It is best to pray when you may disagree with someone else's choice and they refuse to see the truth and make excuses for their bad actions and wrong choices. Don't judge, pray for their release from the captivity. If we don't take the thought captive, the thought rooted will take us captive, that is why we are told to watch with all diligence. *(Proverbs 4:23)*

Always remember, it is God who can change the life in a moment. Use the weapons God has given us to come against strongholds, principalities and powers. God does the work by the power of the Holy Spirit. Love always, pray and follow Gods leading. Stay in peace so you can hear clearly. Be quick to pray and instant in obedience to God and his word.

Chapter Fourteen

Pray at all times

Pray and stand in the gap for the ones that you see headed down a path that you believe will not bring them in to Gods best for them. You can pray they will repent (change their mind) for their sins and ask God to open their eyes, turn them and keep them following the path God has set for them. Ask Him to reveal Himself to them and be close to them and hold fast to them. Ask Him to keep them from the hands of the destroyer and draw them closer to His way and path for them. I believe that even though at times bad things happen that God has made provision and planned the wrong choice in to still be in control of all things. He does after all, hold the keys to Heaven and Hell and there is nothing that He is not Lord over. He is Lord of all, those who acknowledge Him and those who don't. As long as I know God has worked in their life at some point I can be rest assured that "He who began a good work in them will be faithful to complete it". I believe that God knows His own. I believe that as long as I have seen God work in another's life, that even though they may not acknowledge His presence and doings, the work I see Him doing will not have been done in vain and God will complete the work He has begun.

Prayer is the foundation of our relationship with God. It is our conversation with Him. Through prayer is how we get to know Him and build our relationship with Him. Prayer is also our greatest weapon against the enemy.

Ephesians 6:11-13 **Put on the whole armor of God that ye may be able to stand against the wiles of the devil. For we wrestle not against flesh and blood, but against principalities, against powers, against the rulers of the darkness of this world, against spiritual wickedness in high places. Wherefore take unto you the whole armor of God that you may be able to withstand in the evil day, and having done all, to stand. Stand therefore... (KJV)**

2 Corinthians 10:3-5 **For though we walk in the flesh, we do not war after the flesh: For the weapons of our warfare are not carnal, but mighty through God to the pulling down of strong holds; Casting down imaginations, and every high thing that exalts itself against the knowledge of God, and bringing into captivity every thought to the obedience of Christ; (KJV)**

I love the two verses above. They tell us our job here on earth is not to fight with other people but to take the weapons God has given us and fight against the spiritual forces that have attached themselves to our loved ones and others we see in need. Many times you will see something in someone, and our natural reaction is to tell them about it. If they chose not to listen or hear us then we will continue "getting on them" about it, making matters worse by stirring up bad feelings and strife in the house and relationship. This is not God's plan. God doesn't want us arguing and fighting among ourselves. We should do our best to lead them and guide them and correct them, but we should not argue with them if they choose to not to receive the help we have offered. At this point, there is only one thing left we can do, to take up the weapons He has given us and fight a spiritual battle for the person who needs help or is incapable of doing it themselves due to their deception, lack of knowledge or understanding on their part. Most times when I go in to this spiritual battle for my loved ones, honestly, they don't even know until later down the road when they are ready to make the change. If I say anything at all, I just tell them I am praying for them, for things to get better for them.

The following verses tell you our basic armor and weapons. Study it and ask God to reveal to you His word so you can get not only his knowledge, but also His wisdom (which is how to use the knowledge).

Ephesians 6:10-18 **Finally, my brethren, be strong in the Lord, and in the power of his might. Put on the whole armor of God that ye may be able to stand against the wiles of the devil. For we wrestle not against flesh and blood, but against principalities, against powers, against the rulers of the darkness of this world, against spiritual wickedness in high places. Wherefore take unto you the whole armor of God that**

ye may be able to withstand in the evil day, and having done all, to stand. Stand therefore, having your loins girt about with truth, and having on the breastplate of righteousness; and your feet shod with the preparation of the gospel of peace; Above all, taking the shield of faith, wherewith ye shall be able to quench all the fiery darts of the wicked. And take the helmet of salvation, and the sword of the Spirit, which is the word of God: Praying always with all prayer and supplication in the Spirit, and watching thereunto with all perseverance and supplication for all saints; (KJV)

The truth is in the bible for your benefit. Gods' word is true. You must know who you are in Christ and be in right standing with God. This is the only way to put on the breastplate of righteousness. Your feet shod with the preparation of the gospel of peace is to walk in the light of His word, influencing peace among people and the love God has for all mankind, invoking peace wherever you go. Then God says; "Above all", obviously this must be higher on the priority list, your shield of faith. You must have faith, a strong, deep, rooted and grounded faith, nothing wavering. Your faith is what causes you to rise above your circumstances and negative things that people say. Your faith is what makes you overcome all things and why a believer will never except defeat regardless of the circumstances. Through your faith you will be able to put out anything that the evil one throws at you. The helmet of salvation which protects your renewed mind, a mind focused on God and His word and all He gave you at your salvation, and the sword of the spirit, which is the word of God. It is so important to know His word. Without the knowledge you can be easily deceived through twisting and changing even one word of it can change the whole meaning if you are not careful, and it can get you off Gods track. Be sure as you read you are applying it to yourself, not to anyone else. Learning the bible and knowing God is about YOUR relationship with Him, not your spouse, children, or anyone else.

As you come to know God things will be clearer to you. Pray the word. The word works! Find a scripture that covers the area you are fighting and pray that word over the circumstance. Personalize the scriptures, put yours or someone else's name in it, pray it with power and force. You will not see it in the natural realm until it is done in the spiritual realm. Do not lose heart. As Galatians 6:9 says, "And let us not be weary in well doing: for in due season we shall reap, if we faint not" (KJV).

Hebrews 4:12 **For the word of God is quick, and powerful, and sharper than any two-edged sword, piercing even to the dividing asunder of soul and spirit, and of the joints and marrow, and is a discerner of the thoughts and intents of the heart. (KJV)**

Prayer should be part of your daily life. It is your time to commune with God, to have a conversation with Him and get to know Him better. With the forces of God's word and prayer working together (you speaking Gods word) with the power and authority God has given you, and when you combine that with all the other things we have talked about in this book, you will see, that when all these things are in line together, you have now become a powerful force to Gods work and calling for you. As you mature and grow in God, you will learn the incredible power God has given to you.

When you can use all the gifts God has given you, in unison, to their full effect you will find that nothing shall be impossible for you. You will have victory in every area of your life.

Stir up the gift that is within you and learn to walk with God. You will never regret it. You will see how He wishes to honor you, he has placed value within you and He wants to restore you to the place you were originally intended to have. Pray through until you see the victory.

Chapter Fifteen

Follow Gods Heart

We must always strive to follow Gods wishes for us. We must train ourselves to listen to our spirit (something others may call conscience). Our spirit is the part of us that commune with God through the Holy Spirit. We must allow our renewed spirit to dominate and guide us, not our feelings or emotions, not our circumstances. The more sensitive we allow our renewed spirit to be, the better our lives will be.

We are made in Gods image, a triune being. We are a spirit, we have a soul, and we live in a body. The body gives us dominion in this world, which is why Jesus had to come in to this world, in the flesh, so He would have dominion to buy us back through the shedding of His innocent blood. Something we could never do for ourselves. Jesus is Gods flesh, Gods body. We have a spirit which came from God's spirit when He breathed the breath of life into Adam and Eve. Some call this their conscience. That voice within that tells you right from wrong, and as you develop your spirit with the word of God, your spirit will tell you much more in a gradual motion, as you allow it to be developed in the word of God. Your soul is made up of your mind, your will, and your emotions. This is the area we have to work on. We need to renew our mind to the word of God. The word of God is Gods mind, will and emotions on paper for us. You have to line up your will to the word of God, and you must teach your emotions to respond appropriately in accordance with the word of God. This is your battle to win, to bring your mind, will and emotions into obedience of Christ.

2 Corinthians 10:4-5 **For the weapons of our warfare are not carnal, but mighty through God to the pulling down of strong holds; Casting down imaginations, and every high thing that exalts itself against the knowledge of God, and bringing into captivity every thought to the obedience of Christ; (KJV)**

Strong holds are wrong thinking patterns in our mind, imaginations are developed in our mind, and our thoughts are in our mind. We are to pull down, cast down and take captive all the areas of our mind that has itself out of line with God's word. Take control of your every thought and bring it in line with the word of God. Until you can control your mind and what you will allow it to think and meditate on you will have problems controlling anything else in your life.

People tend to react rather than respond. This is two different things. Reactions come from people who allow their emotions to lead the way. Reactions tend to tear down others and usually are not "nice" in nature to another. Responses are usually thought through and give reassurance or build up another and usually are "nice" in nature to another. We must learn to control our emotions and teach ourselves to respond rather than react to situations and circumstances.

God has a clear and concise training manual called the bible to teach us all His ways of righteousness (doing and being right), but you have to take the time to sit with God and allow Him to show you and teach you what you need for the place you are in. Not only that, God knows what is ahead and He wants to prepare you for the future. He knows what you are going to need. Take the time to be with Him and learn His ways. That is a choice you have to make and unfortunately I have seen so many people wait till they have lost it all and are backed in a corner before they will repent and turn to God for help. I don't understand this type of thinking. Some people just keep going around that same mountain over and over again, never learning from their past and blaming everyone else for their life which is a product of their own thoughts and choices. Until this type of person will accept and take responsibility for their life there is nothing you can do but pray and ask God to open their eyes to the truth of His word.

I am the type of person that if I see it is not going to work out well and I am straying, I turn away from it right then because I don't want to go through anything bad happening to me, that I will have to deal with other than what I have no control over and the basic things that life just throws your way just because you are alive. I still don't understand why someone would want to inflict unnecessary pain on themselves, but there are plenty of people out there doing just that. They allow their soul to lead their way through their life. They have not renewed their mind, have not lined up their will with Gods and allow their out of control emotions to lead them through life which is causing them more and more grief, pain and troubles. Unfortunately, until they make their own decision you cannot help them and your help, I believe, can actually be a detriment at times, enabling them not to change. At this point, I pray they reach their bottom so they will turn to God and see the truth. When someone is in this place and they are not teachable, I usually have to pull away from them to some extent, if not totally, so I am not enabling them and I can pray for them rather than bicker with them, but rest assured, if they ask for advice I don't hold back, I am brutally honest and usually end the conversation with "but it's your choice". Upon occasion, I even remind them of the prior choice they made that created their situation to become worse, in an effort, hoping they will see, they are causing their own troubles. You need to know God to really know when you are helping someone or if you are just enabling them to not change, which is really hindering their relationship with God. Only God knows the answer, so pray and wait for Him to answer.

Always do what you know in our heart is the right thing. Make sure it is in line with Gods will (His word). Allow God to reveal to you the appropriate response for the situation you are facing. Find and pray the scripture, be sure your motives are in line with the word and have nothing to do with yourself and what you think, feel or want.

When your prayers (thoughts, words and meditations) and heart are in line with Gods, you will learn what it is to be effective in your prayer life. As long as you live with a clear conscience (clean spirit) and you remain moldable and teachable, and continue to strive toward excellence, able to adjust and adapt, then you are on the right track for God to work and accomplish His purpose for you.

Without Gods leading and guidance through our lives we would continually mess things up. This is why it is so important that we follow after Gods heart and put ourselves in line with His word and will. We have to be able to hear His voice (His word rise up within us) because He is the only one who can tell us our best response to the situations that come our way.

1 Thessalonians 5:14-18 **Now we exhort you, brethren, warn those who are unruly, comfort the fainthearted, uphold the weak, be patient with all. See that no one renders evil for evil to anyone, but always pursue what is good both for yourselves and for all. Rejoice always, pray without ceasing, in everything give thanks; for this is the will of God in Christ Jesus for you. (KJV)**

This new covenant that God has made with us, he says he will put his instructions deep within us and he will write them on our hearts. *(*Read *Jeremiah 31:33, Hebrews 10:16, Romans 2:14)*

This new covenant that we have, is a covenant that **has provided <u>all things</u>** pertaining to life and godliness to us by grace (Gods unmerited favor, a gift), through faith (our believing, trusting and relying on God). Read *Ephesians 2:8-9, 2 Peter 1:3*

The more you know God and understand the Fathers great love for you, the easier it will be for you to follow Gods heart and stay in his peace, protection and rest.

Chapter Sixteen

Stay Focused

Always remember never to compare yourself to another. God is doing a different work in each of us and it is so important to keep moving forward to become the best God has made us to be. Looking at others and the life they lead will only cause you to lose focus and compromise due to the fact that "God lets them get away with it" or does He? Maybe they are in a place of delusion, they have convinced themselves that it is ok, or maybe they are in a place of rebellion. Again, only God knows the motives and intents of a heart. Only He sees the full picture and has their purpose in place. We cannot cop out and compare ourselves to others. If we chose to do that we would be hurting ourselves and denying our own potential and purpose. If we carry an attitude of mediocrity then we will never step into the fullness and blessings God has in store for us. God blesses obedience.

We have to do all we can do to remain focused on Gods goal for our lives. We must press toward the mark, and that mark is to know Him and the power of the resurrection. *(Philippians 3:10)*

Philippians 3:13-14 **Brethren, I count not myself to have apprehended: but this one thing I do, forgetting those things which are behind, and reaching forth unto those things which are before, I press toward the mark for the prize of the high calling of God in Christ Jesus. (KJV)**

God tells us in His word what type of things we should meditate on in the following verse.

Philippians 4:8-9 **Finally, brethren, whatever things are true, whatever things** *are* **noble, whatever things** *are* **just, whatever things** *are* **pure, whatever things** *are* **lovely, whatever things** *are* **of good report, if** *there is* **any virtue and if** *there is* **anything praiseworthy—meditate on these things. The things which you learned and received and heard and saw in me, these do, and the God of peace will be with you. (NKJV)**

If we meditate on the good things, it will help us mentally and emotionally. Our mind will become renewed; we will begin to think differently. We will think in a positive light rather than a negative one. A positive attitude is also what is needed to root your faith. Negative thinking works against your faith and causes your faith to become weak. You want to stay away from negative thoughts and feelings. There is no good that will come from them. We need to focus on the positive, good, pure, and lovely. Stay focused and happier by following Philippians 4:8.

Joshua 1:8 **This Book of the Law shall not depart from your mouth, but you shall meditate in it day and night that you may observe to do according to all that is written in it. For then you will make your way prosperous, and then you will have good success.** (NKJV)

If you keep your focus on God and do as He tells you, He says He will make your way prosperous and you will have good success. There is no maybe or I'll think about it in that verse, He said if you meditate and do according to His word, then YOU will make your way prosperous, and then YOU will have good success.

Notice God says, YOU ....Do, YOU ...Have, the buck starts and stops with you. God tells you all through the bible that YOU are in control, it is your free will, and if you chose to do bad, you will get bad, but if you chose to do good you will get good.

Deuteronomy 30:19 **I call heaven and earth as witnesses today against you, *that* I have set before you life and death, blessing and cursing; therefore choose life, that both you and your descendants may live; (NKJV)**

Life is all about choices and if you want to remain focused, YOU must choose it. Your life is a product of your choices, or your choice not to make a choice, or your choice not to hear, or your choice not to change, or your choice that caused some other consequence. Unless we are a child, there are very few things in this life that our prior choices and current choices did not lead to. Through your choices you have created your life, whether you like it or not, whether you accept it or not, it still remains to be the truth, your life is a product of your choices. Your thinking is a product of your choices. If you want something to change then choose to start making the change. As you consistently make the right choice repeatedly, gradually your life will change, your circumstances will change, and eventually you will be able to look back and see that you have changed your whole life, one choice at a time. Continually choose to stay focused on God and His ways and doing what is right, you will be surprised in a year how far away you are from your old life and your old way of thinking.

    You cannot make choices for anyone else, only for yourself. You can try to help them make a choice and show them the possible results of each of their options, but you cannot make them choose what you want them to or think they should. You can pray and intercede, but you cannot force anyone to make the choice you think they should make and if you try to force them they normally will run away from you as fast as they can. If you are trying to dominate and control another person, your relationship will be a rocky one. No person will live in this circumstance indefinitely. If you are a controlling person, choose to shift that control off everyone else and focus on yourself and your relationship with God. By doing this, you will be taking that negative producing action and turning it in to a positive action. God wants us to have proper control of ourselves and if our focus is on controlling another, then we are not choosing the blessings and life.

Again, you can pray and intercede, and you definitely should, privately, when they are not around, stand in the gap and pray for them. Allow God to prove himself to you. The things that you cannot control give to God, allow Him to fix them. The things you can control, regarding yourself and your relationship with God, take control of and stay focused on you and improving yourself, rather than what everyone around you is doing wrong.

Stay focused on Philippians 4:8 **Finally, brethren, whatever things are true, whatever things *are* noble, whatever things *are* just, whatever things *are* pure, whatever things *are* lovely, whatever things *are* of good report, if *there is* any virtue and if *there is* anything praiseworthy—meditate on these things. (NKJV)**

When we focus on the kingdom principles (Gods ways of doing and being right) with the proper motives (love) we are well under way to seeing Heaven on Earth in your life.

Read *Matthew 6:33*

Lord, help us to keep you and your word first and foremost in our thoughts, words, minds and hearts. In our conscience (thinking, knowing and choosing elements) and sub-conscience (programmed habitual responses based on our training, habits and beliefs). Let us not lean to our own understanding but to look to, lean, trust and rely on you in all things. Thank you for your great love for us and your word and Holy Spirit who lead and guide us in all things. Thank you for your peace and entrance into your rest. Thank you for your protection, goodness and mercy that follow me all the days of my life. Thank you that I shall dwell in the house of the Lord forever.

Chapter Seventeen

Success Assured

Our obedience to him will be richly rewarded. Our attitude determines our altitude (the heights you can go to) with God. Your success is assured if you continuously choose to observe and do all that He commands.

Deuteronomy 28 gives a long list of all the blessing that come upon and overtakes the diligently obedient child of God. It explains that you will be lifted up, favored, blessed, and prosperous it won't matter where you live, what your career, all that matters is that you follow after Him and do what is right by obeying God's word. It is by that obedience that God can pour out all the "blessings" upon you. These blessings will go on to your children as you teach them and bring them up according to His word.

God also tells you in His word the curses that come upon those who won't follow after Him, the confusion and "bad luck" as some call it because they wouldn't chose to do what is right.

Deuteronomy 28 **(Blessings on Obedience)**

1 "Now it shall come to pass, if you diligently obey the voice of the LORD your God, to observe carefully all His commandments which I command you today, that the LORD your God will set you high above all nations of the earth. 2 And all these blessings shall come upon you and overtake you, because you obey the voice of the LORD your God:
3 "Blessed *shall* you *be* in the city, and blessed *shall* you *be* in the country.
4 "Blessed *shall be* the fruit of your body,…….. 12 The LORD will open to you His good treasure, the heavens, to give the rain to your land in its season, and to bless all the work of your hand. You shall lend to many nations, but you shall not borrow. 13 And the LORD will make you the head and not the tail; you shall be above only, and not be beneath, if you heed the commandments of the LORD your God, which I command you today, and are careful to observe *them*. 14 So you shall not turn aside from any of the words which I command you this day, *to* the right or the left, to go after other gods to serve them.

Curses on Disobedience

15 "But it shall come to pass, if you do not obey the voice of the LORD your God, to observe carefully all His commandments and His statutes which I command you today, that all these curses will come upon you and overtake you:
16 "Cursed *shall* you *be* in the city, and cursed *shall* you *be* in the country…….
……. you shall not prosper in your ways; you shall be only oppressed and plundered continually, and no one shall save *you.*30 "You shall betroth a wife, but another man shall lie

with her;…….45 "Moreover all these curses shall come upon you and pursue and overtake you, until you are destroyed, because you did not obey the voice of the LORD your God, to keep His commandments and His statutes which He commanded you. 46 And they shall be upon you for a sign and a wonder, and on your descendants forever. 47 "Because you did not serve the LORD your God with joy and gladness of heart, for the abundance of everything,……….. (NKJV)

And it goes on to verse 61!!! Basically, nothing you do will work, you will not be prosperous, your marriage will be a mess due to adultery, if you don't divorce, and this is just a small portion of what you are opening yourself and your family up to! Thankfully, Jesus put all of the above into perspective for us in the New Testament.

Matthew 22:37-40 **37 Jesus said to him, " *'You shall love the LORD your God with all your heart, with all your soul, and with all your mind.* 38 This is *the* first and great commandment. 39 And *the* second *is* like it: *'You shall love your neighbor as yourself.* 40 On these two commandments hang all the Law and the Prophets." (NKJV)**

    Our success is assured if we chose obedience, or our defeat is assured if we choose disobedience. It is just that simple. If you want to be successful, be obedient. Choose to know God and to follow His will and ways and you are assured success.

    God is loving and merciful, if you have been living a life that your do not want to reap the full consequences of, then turn away from what you have been doing wrong, ask Jesus to cleanse you with His blood, pray for crop failure and start doing what is right. As long as you are in your body you have dominion and have the right to choose and to change your mind and make it right, until your body is dead, at that point you have lost your right and the choice you made while alive is the choice you will have to live with throughout eternity.

We never know when our time will be up and it is best to make your choice now and accept Christ, His forgiveness and learn about His loving-kindness. For some of us the time to make the choice is now, there is no later on down the road. Some of us may die unexpectedly later today, or tomorrow. Don't take the chance, make your choice now. Once you accept Him and start living for Him, you will finally know what "fullness of life" is.

Don't wait! If you haven't already accepted Christ, accept Him now! If you put off the choice of accepting Him, then your lack of choice is your choice. Do not be deceived. God loves you and wants to make things better in your life. Won't you allow Him into your heart to help you? I promise, if you choose Him, you will never be alone again, He will always be with you, He will never leave you or forsake you.

Chapter Eighteen

Thoughts and Words

If we refuse to "go to bad places" mentally and replace those questionable thoughts with Gods thoughts and words He will raise us up above and beyond all we can think and imagine. This is not something that happens overnight. This comes through determination, testing and perseverance. It is something that can only be accomplished through believing God at His word. If you really don't believe, then you won't continue in the thing until it manifests. You will give up due to negative, deceptive thoughts and words that come to you. You must be sure that you align your thoughts and words with what the word says your response and meditations should be. Without proper knowledge and the wisdom (which is a gift from God and how to use the knowledge) the bible holds, you will be hard pressed to stay focused.

We need to be sure that our thoughts are on things that are good, pure, lovely and of good report. If there be any praise or virtue, think on these things. Be sure that you appreciate things. Don't allow things to pass by with unspoken thanks.

The bible has much to say about your thoughts and words. This is an extremely important area to master in order to have victory in your life.

Psalm 34:12-14 **Who *is* the man *who* desires life, and loves *many* days, that he may see good? Keep your tongue from evil, and your lips from speaking deceit.
Depart from evil and do good; Seek peace and pursue it. (NKJV)**

Psalm 35:28 **And my tongue shall speak of Your righteousness and of Your praise all the day long. (NKJV)**

James 1:26 **If anyone among you thinks he is religious, and does not bridle his tongue but deceives his own heart, this one's religion is useless. (NKJV)**

James 3 **(The Untamable Tongue)**

**1 My brethren, let not many of you become teachers, knowing that we shall receive a stricter judgment. 2 For we all stumble in many things. If anyone does not stumble in word, he *is* a perfect man, able also to bridle the whole body. 3 Indeed, we put bits in horses' mouths that they may obey us, and we turn their whole body. 4 Look also at ships: although they are so large and are driven by fierce winds, they are turned by a very small rudder wherever the pilot desires. 5 Even so the tongue is a little member and boasts great things.
See how great a forest a little fire kindles! 6 And the tongue *is* a fire, a world of iniquity. The tongue is so set among our members that it defiles the whole body, and sets on fire the course of nature; and it is set on fire by hell. 7 For every kind of beast and bird, of reptile and creature of the sea, is tamed and has been tamed by mankind. 8 But no man can tame the tongue. *It is* an unruly evil, full of deadly poison. 9 With it we**

bless our God and Father, and with it we curse men, who have been made in the similitude of God. 10 Out of the same mouth proceed blessing and cursing. My brethren, these things ought not to be so.(NKJV)

It tells you above that your words set on fire the course of nature, your words determine your life. That is why people say, "You will have what you say", and it is the truth – the way you speak about yourself and your circumstances – your words set the course of your future life. This is why it is so important to watch your words. The words you choose to blurt out of your mouth set things in motion for you to receive what you have spoken.

Do you constantly speak negatively about your life and circumstances? Think about all the words you put in motion regarding your life years ago, now look at your life presently, are you reaping the response to your words? Some people walk around professing, "life sucks" and years later, guess what it really does for them. They brought that into existence themselves and created a life that really does suck. Try and tell them this and they won't hear it- it is always someone else's fault. They choose to become bitter rather than better. God says, "out of the abundance of the heart the mouth speaks". That means that your words show you what is in your heart. If you want to know what is in your heart, listen to your words. Your words reflect what you have stored and filled your heart with. That is why God says to think on things that are good, pure, lovely and of good report, if there be anything of virtue and praiseworthy meditate on these things.

When you meditate on the bad things of life you are filling your heart with bad things and your speech will reflect these bad things. Basically you are starting a cycle for more bad and worse to happen because you didn't learn, as I did when I was younger, "If you don't have something nice to say, don't say anything at all". The word of God takes it even further and says not only don't say it, don't even think on it (meditate). If you put bad in to your life, you will get bad out of your life. It is the law of nature. God also says as a man thinks in his heart, so is he. That is telling you that as you choose to view your life – that is what it will be for you.

If you have two people and exactly the same thing happens to them, let's say one chooses to view it negatively and he becomes depressed, down trodden and life becomes more and more miserable for him because that is the way he choose to see it. He lives a defeated life because he chooses to think and speak the negative things. The second person chooses to view the circumstance as positively as they could and make the best of their circumstances and when they couldn't see any good they chose not to think on it and make the best of what they could anyway. This second person's life will get better, they will overcome the circumstance and have a victorious life because of the choice they made to follow Gods way of dealing with things and finding and thinking on the good that may come out of it.

Simple Steps To A Better Life

Until you realize the power that is in your thoughts and words, and take the necessary steps to line yourself up with the word of God and His ways, you will never be able to live the life God wants you to have. You will constantly sabotage your life and inflict yourself with negative living which will cause you to always see defeat in your life. If you walk around murmuring, grumbling and complaining, wining and unsatisfied with everything then you will continue to see more dissatisfaction in your life from your own words.

If you are ready to make the change to better your life, pray for crop failure and start speaking the word and good into your life. Change the way you think about things and the words you speak and you will change your life. Remember your life is the way YOU have made it and the way YOU perceive it. Take responsibility for where you are and if you don't like the way you have made it, then change it through changing your thoughts and words to good ones.

As you meditate on the word of God and change your thoughts to line up with the word, you are renewing your mind to the word and through this process you are able to retrain your thoughts and responses. This will form new habits, perceptions and feelings to follow as you continue in the process. As the inner man (unseen) is renewed it will overflow to the outer (seen) man. As your thinking is changed in each area there will be definite differences you will be able to see in the natural man.

For example, as you renew your mind in the area of Gods love for you, as the belief is built and burned into your heart (subconscience) the results of that new belief cause new feelings and perceptions of yourself to emerge that correspond with your new belief. Many times knowing and believing you are loved will change your perception of yourself by giving you a greater value and esteem. For some it may get rid of all feelings of insecurity, depression and abandonment once they have the knowing of Gods love for them personally. Those bad or negative feelings many times will be replaced with feelings of security, joy, loved and wanted feelings and when you have these new feelings, they will cause your life to follow a good and positive flow. You will see that your responses are more uplifting, without even thinking about it eventually, because you have reprogramed you subconscience to respond in the nature of God and according to his word. Just like anything, once you have done it enough repetitiously, eventually it is a habit and you wont even have to think, it will just flow out of you naturally.

Chapter Nineteen

Be Determined

Nothing worth having in life is usually easy to obtain. The better things in life require diligence, consistency and determination. It is not usually easy initially. Simple, yes, Gods ways are simple, easy, no, it is never easy to change yourself after the many years you have embedded yourself into your life habits and the way you have chosen to program your brain to think and respond. Along the way, your compilation of thoughts and words have made you and designed the way you think and your actions and every other facet of your life. You must be determined that you want a change and continue encouraging yourself along the way with good thoughts and words. You have to pay attention to your thoughts and words and measure them against the word of God. Are your thoughts and words, good, pure, lovely of good report? If they are not then you have to determine to correct them. The easiest way to correct an improper thought is to replace it with what the word of God says about it. For example, if you hear yourself think or say, "I am losing my mind", you should immediately replace it with, "I have the mind of Christ". I replaced the negative thought with a positive from 1 Corinthians 2:16.

Romans 12:2 says, **And be not conformed to this world: but be ye transformed by the renewing of your mind, that ye may prove what is that good, and acceptable, and perfect, will of God. (KJV)**

You are to be transformed by the renewing of your mind. Your battlefield is in your soul – your mind, will and emotions - your thoughts and words are part of your soul and if you want to be transformed you have to renew your mind. To do this you will have to get rid of all thoughts and words that go against Gods word and replace them with thoughts and words that are aligned with God's word.

You will have to determine that God's word is true and that it is the final authority in your life. You cannot just accept parts and pieces of His word. You have to determine that Gods word, in its entirety is true, whether you like it or not, whether you "feel" it or not and whether you think you want to believe it or not. Even when something seems far from my understanding, I chose to believe it, even if I don't understand it, and I ask the Holy Spirit to teach my spirit because then my spirit (conscience) can help direct my soul.

Everything takes time. You will not know it all over night and no one expects you to. Walking with God is a day by day walk and we will never know it all, not while we are on this earth. You will be in a continual learning process. We all are a work (Gods work) in progress. No one on this earth knows everything about God. We are all at different levels on the way to the place God has appointed for us. What God calls one to do, may not be what He calls another to. Don't allow yourself to become discouraged. Be determined to reach the goal God has for you.

So many people cut themselves off from God's blessings because they won't continue for the duration. When resistance comes they give up. They haven't determined or convinced themselves that if they stay teachable God will take them to the place He has for them. I understand that you may find it hard to walk in Gods ways. People may have things to say and they will not understand because it goes against the world's ways of doing things, the way they "know you to be". They expect a certain reaction from you and you have never let them down from acting that way before. Now, all of a sudden it seems, you are not taking your "normal" reaction and instead you are responding, differently, lovingly and understandingly. Some will work on you to bring you back to the way you were, but you can't let them trick or manipulate you into regressing.

You will have to be determined. God has great things ahead for you and you must be determined in order to achieve all the blessings He has for you. The people you acquaint with may say or do things to try to get you back to their thinking, that old way of thinking you used to have. When you have aligned yourself to follow God and go against your old self, initially you may feel that everything is coming against you because the only objective is to get you to give up, cave in, quit and take the "easy" well known, comfortable path that you have been in for years. You must resolve to be determined and not allow yourself to fall back into the life you left behind when you accepted Christ and by all means, if you have then repent and get out quick and press on toward Gods plan for you. The longer you walk with God and the more right decisions you acquire along the way, the easier it will become to remain in Gods way for you.

    I cannot stress enough that you have to be determined that you want Gods best for you and for all those your life is intertwined with. As you chose the best and walk in Gods best, you will receive Gods best, then you will be able to give Gods best to others.

    You can't give something you don't have. You can't teach your children what you don't first know and own yourself. Be determined to know God so you can have the greatest gift and value in mankind to give to others.

Chapter Twenty

Have Faith

Romans 5:1-2 **Therefore, since we have been made right in God's sight by faith, we have peace with God because of what Jesus Christ our Lord has done for us. Because of our faith, Christ has brought us into this place of undeserved privilege where we now stand, and we confidently and joyfully look forward to sharing God's glory (NLT)**

This surety and determination is a form of faith. Although faith comes in many forms these are two qualities that faith will always have. After all "faith is the substance of things hoped for, the evidence of things you have yet to see" and "without faith it is impossible to please God". This surety and determination is also a form of believing. Without them you cannot be a believer. You can't believe in something you have rejected, you would wind up wavering all over the place without the determination of knowing what you know. Once you know something and you know that you know, and then no one will ever be able to talk you out of it. At this point, it will have to be your own judgment call, when you judge yourself against the word of God.

Your faith is your root system. It is the part that anchors you in to Gods word and world. Without faith it is impossible to please Him because without faith you will not claim what is rightfully yours – you will just accept whatever comes as "your lot in life". Without faith you will not be able to step out and accomplish what God has called you to do.

Romans 12:3 says, **For I say, through the grace given unto me, to every man that is among you, not to think of himself more highly than he ought to think; but to think soberly, according as God hath dealt to every man the measure of faith.(KJV)**

God states that you have faith. He has dealt to every man the measure of faith. Some people have distorted Gods intention for faith. They have faith in the negative and bad, which works against them and brings to pass their own worst fears due to their thoughts, words and faith that it will be bad. If this is where your faith is, you must turn it around and use it as God intended, for your own good.

God wants us full of faith, faith that He is in control, faith that He knows our outcome, faith in His word, faith in good being able to come about even though circumstances look bad. Using your faith correctly can make you whole, healed, saved, purified, righteous, sanctified, and you will be able to obtain all God has already set aside for you. It is up to you to develop your faith.

Luke 17:6 says, **and the Lord said, if ye had faith as a grain of mustard seed, ye might say unto this sycamore tree, be thou plucked up by the root, and be thou planted in the sea; and it should obey you. (KJV)**

A mustard seed is the tiniest of all seeds and if you had even that small amount of faith, a tree should obey you. That is the truth, whether we can make it happen or not, is a problem with us, not with the word, the word is true and we now have a goal, to establish our faith so that we know, we have the power in our faith to accomplish what we say.

Study the book of Romans in the bible. You will learn much about faith. It is by faith that we stand and await the promises of God. We walk by faith and not by sight. We don't look at the circumstances or what we see. Our actions are governed by faith and by the things we cannot see. The just shall live by faith. Your faith is a comfort to you when you go through adverse situations in life. As you develop your faith and the more you are rooted and grounded, the greater joy you will be able to maintain through adverse situations.

Never allow anything to stagger your faith. Match all your thoughts and words with the word of God. Jesus came to fulfill the law and now, the life we live is in the faith of what Jesus has done for us. His work is finished, just waiting for us to lay hold in faith and take what He set aside for us.

Your faith should be accompanied with power. As you increase in faith you should be increasing in power and you should be seeing greater and greater victory in your life as your faith is developed and set in motion.

Keep the faith and do not waver in your mind and you will be able to live successfully and victoriously in Jesus.

Chapter Twenty-One

Stability Established

There is no one who will be able to change your mind on something you have faith and believe in whether good or bad. This is the stance that we must have toward Gods word (the bible) we must read it until we have allowed it to saturate our mind and has changed our thinking to agree with the word. Then, as God moves in our lives and our experiences mount we will eventually be unshakable, immovable steady and stable.

How many people today, in this day and age, waver and are wish-wash, blowing with whatever wind happens to blow at the moment. People pleasers are this way. They adjust and adapt to whoever they are around so as not to upset anyone and "fit in". They usually fear rejection and that is why they work so hard to keep people happy with them. They cannot handle that there may be someone on the planet that may not care for them. Should they realize, they then become obsessed with making amends and doing all they can do to please the offended party. We are not here to please men. We will never be able to become stable when we are trying to please people. We are here to please God.

We have to be comfortable with who God made us to be, who we are and who we are going to develop into, in Christ. The only one that we need to please is God. You will find that you will only become established and stable through knowing God and following His ways.

We are called to love, unconditionally, but loving someone does not always please them. Sometimes you have to love them enough to let them know that things they do are unacceptable and that you do not approve, and it is because of your love for them, that you tell them the truth for their own wellbeing and future.

If you love someone you will not yes them to death or join in for a pity party with them. If you love them, you will do all you can do to lead them and guide them into a place that will make their life better, if they will receive it. It is not love to leave someone deceived in their own delusion.

We need to show stability in our lives so others can see it. Inconsistencies on our part do not show stability, whether those inconsistencies are with ourselves, our children or anyone else. We have to be a good example and show our children and the others in our lives that regardless of the circumstance we will do our part to fulfill what God has required of us, regardless of what another thinks.

As you go through life you may come to a place where your child has acted in a way that is inappropriate toward another, just totally wrong actions were displayed. Many people automatically believe that you will "side" with your child, but the truth is, if you love your child you will tell him his inappropriate behavior and action and tell him it isn't right and not to do it anymore because it is wrong and unacceptable behavior. At this point you will probably go to the person the offense was committed against and apologize and have your child apologize. This is the right and proper thing to do. If we allow them to believe this inappropriate behavior is acceptable under any circumstances then we are hurting our children and their future.

You should be watching for that behavior, so you can be consistent in your efforts of teaching them the right thing. If your child sees that they can do it one time to someone and "get away with it" then they will continually try to "get away with it" and it is the same if both parents do not have the children conform to the same standards and reinforce or back each other up. When a child thinks that there are things that they can "get away with" under supervision of either parent, then you are doing them, the children, injustice. They become confused and learn to manipulate and you actually are hurting them by not fulfilling your duty as a parent.

Proverbs 22:6 says, **Train up a child in the way he should go: and when he is old, he will not depart from it. (KJV)**

Deuteronomy 6:7 says, **You shall teach them diligently to your children, and shall talk of them when you sit in your house, when you walk by the way, when you lie down, and when you rise up. (NKJV)**

It is our responsibility to teach and train our children Gods ways and how to be stable, loving and to do what is right in all situations that may come their way, regardless if we class them as fair or exceptional in circumstance.

Proverbs 23:13-14 says**, Do not withhold correction from a child, For *if* you beat him with a rod, he will not die. You shall beat him with a rod, and deliver his soul from hell. (NKJV)**

If we do not teach our children then we have done them a great injustice. We must be diligent and in Deuteronomy 6:7 you see that it should be consistent, all day, every day, teaching and training is your responsibility regardless of the situation or circumstances. You are to do all you can do. Excusing your children from seeing their wrongs and not correcting them, will allow them to enter into a delusional state and they will be deceived into thinking that their behavior is acceptable and correct when it totally is unacceptable.

It is always easier to train them initially then to try and break a bad habit later. Do yourself and your children the favor of being a parent and teacher to them. When they are older there will be plenty of time to be their friend. They will understand, as the circle of life continues and they are raising their own children and they will thank you for teaching them, so they don't have unruly children, and you all will be together in Heaven for eternity.

I know there are times when the parents are not together and the children are getting two totally different perspectives on correction. They may be able to do something in the presence of one parent that the other won't allow. I assure you, that you do all you can do, to teach them to the best of your ability, with all diligence and consistency, that they act appropriately at all times, understand what is expected from them and explain to them that God is watching them all the time, they aren't getting away with it, if they know better and chose not to do better, they will have to answer to God themselves for that, if you have taught them about God, they will think twice before doing wrong.

Do the best you can do, be sure they know you love them, and God loves them, explain the consequences of wrong choices, pray and let God work out the rest when they are not in your presence. Of course, if you are told that they were misbehaving when they were not with you, then you cannot ignore it, you must deal with them as if they did it in your presence. If they see you shrug off your responsibility to correct and teach them because you weren't there to see it, knowing you were told, and then they will continue to play that card out and misbehave until they are no longer getting away with it. Pray for your children, have faith that the good will overcome the evil.

Simple Steps To A Better Life

When the child is old enough, they will make their own choices, and you will only be held accountable for your own actions and ways that you have taught them. Once they are of age of knowing then they will be held accountable for their own choices. If you truly love you children you will train them in the ways of righteousness and not send them into the world without the knowledge that is needed, not only to survive, but also to have a good, full, joyful life.

Establish stability in your children from the beginning. Give them the gift of your love and knowledge. Don't allow them to walk around in darkness, without having Jesus to be rooted and grounded in. Teach them that Jesus is their rock and fortress and all the benefits that come with Him.

Be open with your children, talk with them, they understand more than you think. By the age of 5 a child has already put many of their personality traits to work for them. Help them to make good choices, teach them and train them in the way they should go right from the beginning. Allow then to suffer the consequences of their actions at a young age and as they are older they will already be trained to follow after good consequences because they will already understand that their choice will bring them either good or bad. Teach them to go beyond the decision to see the repercussions of their choices ahead of time. Your children are worth the effort and you will have the reward of seeing them live in victory. Help them to have stability established in their lives.

Chapter Twenty-Two

You Are Special

God made each of us special and unique. There is no one like you. You are an original, a work of God's hands. He has made you for a special purpose.

Many times we have a hard time and don't see ourselves the way God sees us. This is why it is so important to study the word of God so you can begin and grow into seeing yourself properly the way God sees you.

John 1:12-13 says, **But as many as received him, to them gave he power to become the sons of God, even to them that believe on his name: Which were born, not of blood, nor of the will of the flesh, nor of the will of man, but of God. (KJV)**

Romans 8:14 says, **for as many as are led by the Spirit of God, they are the sons of God. (KJV)**

This is saying that if we have received Christ and our spirit has been reborn then we have the power to be the sons of God and if the Spirit of God leads us then we are the sons of God.

Do you realize that from the beginning we were to have dominion and rule over this earth?

Genesis 1: 26 **And God said, Let us make man in our image, after our likeness: and let them have dominion over the fish of the sea, and over the fowl of the air, and over the cattle, and over all the earth, and over every creeping thing that creepeth upon the earth. 27So God created man in his own image, in the image of God created he him; male and female created he them. 28And God blessed them, and God said unto them, Be fruitful, and multiply, and replenish the earth, and subdue it: and have dominion over the fish of the sea, and over the fowl of the air, and over every living thing that moveth upon the earth. 29And God said, Behold, I have given you every herb bearing seed, which is upon the face of all the earth, and every tree, in the which is the fruit of a tree yielding seed; to you it shall be for meat. 30And to every beast of the earth, and to every fowl of the air, and to every thing that creepeth upon the earth, wherein there is life, I have given every green herb for meat: and it was so. (KJV)**

From the beginning we were to have dominion and be the ruler of the earth. We lost that, but Jesus gave us entrance to rule and reign again, through the shedding of His blood and our acceptance of what He did for us.

1 Peter 2:_9 **But ye are a chosen generation, a royal priesthood, an holy nation, a peculiar people; that ye should shew forth the praises of him who hath called you out of darkness into his marvelous light; (KJV)**

We are royalty. We are Priests. He says we are His own special people. We have to know who we are, so we can teach our children rightly who they are. Are we raising our children as royalty? Do we understand what that consists of? It does not mean that they get everything they want and always get their way. It means that they are raised with greater moral fiber and they have notable excellence, a regal character. Are we teaching them to rule and reign? Do they know that they have a great inheritance and they are in training to be leaders? Are we teaching them how to exercise the supreme authority and power they have in Jesus? Have you given them the knowledge they need and the wisdom necessary to accomplish all God requires for their inheritance to be given to them?

1 Corinthians 6:17 says, **But he that is joined unto the Lord is one spirit. (KJV)**

We are one with Jesus. Our children need to understand and be taught that life doesn't revolve around a single person or around themselves; they need to know that there is a higher plan, you have to be sure they understand there is a greater responsibility we each have, and that responsibility is more than just to ourselves and our pleasures. For we all think and act like life revolves around us, which is true to an extent, there is no one like us and there are gifts that we carry that others of us do not. That is what makes us special, individuals and unique.

Simple Steps To A Better Life

When we remember that all our gifts are from God and He will give them out as He sees fit, knowing that tends to keep us more humble. After all it really isn't us; it again comes back to God and what He has done, similar to someone who was born into royalty. They are not in that position because of their efforts or because of anything they did; they are in that position because of who their father is.

Our Father is God. We have a great inheritance; because of Him we have a great responsibility, as does any prince or princess. We must be taught to conduct ourselves a certain way and think on things in a larger perspective. We must learn to serve others and be fair, not hot headed or self-seeking. We should always be looking for changes we can make to improve our kingdom.

Jesus is our example and we, through our choosing of joining with Him, we are called to learn from Him, be like Him, love like Him.

Until you know just how special you are, you will have a hard time raising your children as you should, treating them and showing them how valuable and precious they are, and how important it is for them to be well mannered, helpful, clean, loving, diligent, fair, honest, kind, respectful, giving their best in all areas of their life, trustworthy, determined, motivated, conscientious, knowledgeable, understanding, a good speaker, as well as, a good listener, has a proper attitude and outlook on life, full of wisdom in all matters pertaining to life and godliness, able to respond to a person's question in a moment's notice, and the list can go on and on.

If your children are older, and there are areas that you feel they could develop in through this book and the knowledge it carries, then don't despair. Get a copy of this book for them. I plan that each and every family member of mine will have their own copy of this book so they can use it for reference throughout their lives and it is my intent, that this book be passed down to all the generations that follow, for their reference as well. It is too important to their welfare to chance that something is overlooked.

God has given us the Word and Holy Spirit to teach us all his ways. It is important that we teach our children the importance and blessing that come form our knowledge, understanding and personal relationship with God. Each of us has a unique relationship with our Father. We hear him speak to us through His Word and in our conscience. That still small voice within you that wants to lead you and guide you to do all the right things. Unfortunately, too many have stifled the spirit through ignoring it, choosing opposite of it or drowning it out through worry, stress and the cares of this world, all distractions to keep you from hearing Christ in you.

In Gods word you have everything necessary to develop a good, close and intimate relationship with God. When God talks to you, be sure to hearken unto the voice of his word. Be obedient and always remember that His spoken work will always agree with his written word and it will never hurt another. All Gods ways are good and filled with love. If its not good or filled with love it is not from God. If it would hurt someone else it is not from God. God calls us to love our neighbor as our self. He would never tell us to do anything that would harm. We must remember that God loves all and He wishes that no one would perish but all would come to eternal life. (Read *1 Timothy 2)*

YOU are special. God made you special and unique, one of a kind, an original. There is no one else like you. In Christ, you are royalty and you have a great inheritance coming your way, be sure you and your family are trained and prepared to receive it. Renew your mind by retraining your thoughts and words and in the consistency and diligence you will successfully reprogram your heart. You will see you are being changed into the image of Christ. Read *2 Corinthians 3, Romans.*

Chapter Twenty - Three

Be Grateful

I am so grateful for the great things Jesus has done and prepared for us. We need to be thankful and show appreciation to others for all they do for us. We need to be thankful for all God has given us. The protection He has given over our families and us.

"Enter His gates with thanksgiving in our hearts and we enter His courts with praise. This is the day that the Lord has made I will rejoice for He has made me glad."

This should be a mindset, an attitude, not only toward God but in all of life. We have to be sure that we are thankful for all things. Thankful for breathing and the food you eat, the family you have, the work you can do, the help you can give and if you take the time to think about it there is a whole host of other things to be thankful for. I am thankful for the health of all my family members. As you consider all the blessings that God has bestowed on you, I am sure that you will come up with quite a list of your own.

"Give thanks with a grateful heart". This should always be on the top of the list. Rejoice and be glad, be exceedingly joyful. Gratefulness is one step toward living in joy. Your attitude toward life and God will lead you in a direction, a good attitude will lead you in a good path and a bad attitude will lead you down a bad path. Thankfulness helps you to see things in a good way.

We need to express gratitude, show that we are pleased concerning all things, but especially when a comfort has been given, or for a discomfort we had, has been relieved or alleviated.

We must train ourselves to show feelings of gratitude and appreciation not only to God but to people as well. We should evaluate the value, significance and worth of the things we have been given and are offered. We should be fully aware and be able to recognize efforts by another, whether it is from God or man. We should point out the good that we see around us and in others and the good that comes our way and happens to us.

By showing our appreciation, we are showing a type of respect, a regard, esteem, honor, and recognition. There is a great significance to doing this, not only for you but for others around you, who hear you as well. We will reap the benefits of thinking on good things and the person it is toward is glad to know that they were able to help you, but it also is a seed that you have planted in other people's hearts, to also show that same type of thankfulness.

We hope that all the lives we touch on a daily basis are able to see the good things in life, and that our focus on these things (these "seeds" we plant), will carry over to others and God will be able to cause those seeds to grow in their heart.

We want our sphere of influence to be that of good, not evil. Feeling grateful is not enough, we must show it, so others will see and be able to learn, or so that seeds can be planted. All good emotions should be shown and expressed so another can have joy through your expression. Notice, I said "good" and I also gave you the response that this expression should bring, joy (a glad and happy heart, reverence, respect). So, if what you want to express is not going to bring a "good" result, and build up, then you should be careful expressing it.

All through the book of Psalms we are told to rejoice, rejoice and again I say rejoice. This is the day that the Lord has made, I will rejoice and be glad in it. Rejoicing will bring joy. As we understand that we have control and the dominion over our self, that we should be able to tell ourselves to do a certain thing and act a certain way, then we will learn to be in joy regardless of our circumstances. We will no longer focus on the natural (seen) world but we will keep ourselves set on the higher (unseen) world and kingdom principles. Seeing all things from that vantage point, with all things under your feet should also cause a grateful heart and cause joy to rise. Knowing we are loved and protected by God should also cause a grateful heart and our joy to rise.

Do you see how God made this all works together? As we follow Gods direction, we grow and become closer to him and his image, line upon line, precept upon precept and we also enjoy our life more. We have more peace, more joy, and more patience, more of anything we choose to give attention to and grow in our life. Our God is truly an Awesome God.

Thank you Father for all your goodness and mercy you have bestowed upon us. We have so very much to be grateful for. Open our eyes to the magnitude of your greatness. Let the Lord be magnified in my life always.

Chapter Twenty-Four

Stay in Peace

There are many things in life that will try and keep us upset and distracted from living the way God our Father intended. We must trust in God and the finished work of Jesus so deeply that we cast all our cares on God because we know He cares for us. Read *1 Peter 5:7*. It takes trust to not follow and figure out the natural. Our minds want to think and dwell on the circumstance until we have it figured out. During this process is where you will lose your peace if you aren't careful.

There is a natural desire to want to figure everything out and see the end result before it happens, but there are times and circumstances that you will not ever figure out or see a way that it will turn out for your good. This is where you must learn to trust God and cast the care onto Him to take care of for you. Only then, when you have truly given the issue to God will you be able to have and remain in peace.

Jesus said in *John 14:27*, He left us peace, not the world's peace but true peace that in the midst of everything going wrong and chaos all around us, peace would still be the atmosphere within us. This is so true, awesome and amazing. When you truly live this, you will understand. It is real. It is available to you. You must choose it and continuously make the conscience effort to cast the care onto God, not think of it at all, other than when the thought comes, you would have the knowing within you, that God has got it and will take care of you.

John 14:27 **Peace I leave with you, my peace I give unto you: not as the world giveth, give I unto you. Let not your heart be troubled, neither let it be afraid. (KJV)**

Jeremiah 29:11 **For I know the thoughts I think toward you saith the Lord, thoughts of peace and not of evil, to give you an expected end. (KJV)**

I like the version that says," I give you a hope and a future". We must remember that God knows the end. In His presence there is no time. He already knows every choice we make and has provided us with a way to escape. Read *1 Corinthians 10:13* and *Philippians 4*, which says the peace of God that passes ALL understanding will also keep your heart and mind. Our job is to bring every thought captive to the knowledge of Christ (the anointed one and His anointing). Think on God and the good. Don't let anything replace the truth of the Word in your thinking.

    Don't allow the distractions of life to take your peace. You have the power and authority. You make the decision what you will think and believe, what you will let in and throw out. You are the guardian of your thoughts and your thoughts become actions and your actions become your life. That's why its true that as a man thinks, so is he.

You and your life are a product of your thought and beliefs. When you line up your thoughts with Gods Word and believe in the Finished Work of Jesus, you will find you have access to a whole new life in Christ and you have the ability to live by a totally different set of standards and principles that many of us call Kingdom principles. As you grow in grace and your soul (mind, will and emotions) prospers everything else in your life will prosper. Nothing can stop Gods Word from accomplishing all it was set out to do except unbelief. Because of unbelief even Jesus could do no mighty works for the people in his hometown *(Matthew 13:58)*. Their unbelief stopped them from being able to receive all that Jesus was there to give them.

All the gifts of God come the same way; we hear the Word, faith comes *(Romans 10:17)*, we choose to believe *(Hebrews 11:6)*, we ask believing we have received *(Mark 11:24-26, John 14:11-15)* and we thank and praise Him *(Philippians 4:6-7, Colossians 3:17, 1 Thessalonians 5:18)* knowing manifestation is on its way.

Yes, that simple. Easy? No. This goes against what we have been taught. We have been taught to follow after the natural world and circumstances, what we see, feel, smell, etc. God says we are to live according to the unseen, by faith, because it is the higher life and laws that rule and cause manifestation into the natural. We have the same ability to create our life by our thoughts and words, just as God did in the beginning and continues to do. Very few have matured enough to walk and live the life God intended for us. Obtaining has much to do with our ability to stay in peace. The more we are able to have peace shows your trust level. If you don't have peace then you aren't trusting God or haven't cast the care to Him. Worry, stress and panic attacks are all opposite side of the coin of peace. If you are experiencing any of these, peace is what you need and trust in God is the only way to get it.

Make the decision to cast ALL your cares on God, choose to trust Him and His great love for you, and then you will find His peace that passes all understanding will flood your soul (mind, will, and emotions). I promise you, the experience is like nothing you have ever imagined and this deep inner peace brings with it joy unspeakable.

Let peace be your umpire and stay in peace always.

Chapter Twenty-Five

Enter His Rest

Hebrews 4:9-11 **There remaineth therefore a rest to the people of God. For he that is entered into his rest, he also has ceased from his own works, as God did from his. Let us labour therefore to enter into that rest, lest any man fall after the same example of unbelief.**

Entering into the rest of God…in my mind, is to be under his wing. I like that picture better because it is more personal to me than running into his strong tower or running into his fortress. I enjoy living under the shadow of His wing.

We will not be able to enter the rest of God without certain kingdom principles in place; faith that works by love (*Galatians 5:6)*, thoughts captive to the obedience of Christ *(2 Corinthians 10:5)*, the tongue tamed (James 3), pretty much everything this book has touched on.

Rest comes after you have developed your trust and live in the peace of God. Rest comes when you believe His word, when you believe He loves you *(John 3:16, 15:13)*, when you believe nothing shall harm you (*Luke 10:19*), when you believe you dwell in the secret place of the Most High, when you believe God has angels watching over you (*Psalm 91*), when you believe, lean, trust in and rely on God, Jesus and their finished work and receive all your gifts of the covenant of grace.

When you realize we can make choices that will put us in the position to receive and live life the way God originally intended before sin entered the world and the fall of man…wow! That is exactly what Jesus did for us. We have been restored and made whole by the blood of Jesus. In Him is our life. Just as Holy Spirit was with Jesus, He is with us who are born again believers.

When our thoughts are Gods thoughts, and our words are Gods words and we believe whole-heartedly we will be astonished at the ease we have in life. None of us have arrived, we are all a work in progress but I have been blessed with glimpses and moments of what's ahead.

When we command our life from the higher, the lower must conform. Where there is struggle, strife and disharmony there is no trust in God, no faith, no peace and no rest. These things don't come from God and we shouldn't entertain them in our lives. They come from pride (*Proverbs 13:10*). We must retrain ourselves to live from the higher (unseen) rather than the lower (sensual) nature. Only then will we be able to remain in rest regardless of what it appears in the natural is happening.

We need to see things from Gods perspective, looking down (*Ephesians 2:4-10*), knowing it is all under our feet

(Ephesians 1:22) and only temporary *(2 Corinthians 4:18)*. You must believe that God has got you and will not let go *(John 10:28-30)*. You have great worth and value to him *(Isaiah 43, John 3:16)*. You are his child. He made you *(Jeremiah 1:5, Psalm 82:6, Galatians 3:26-27)*. You are an heir and joint heir with Christ Jesus *(Romans 8:13-19)*

We know we would not allow harm to come to our children because we love them. How much more is God, who IS love, not going to allow harm to those of us who have chosen to hide under the shadow of His wing and rest in Him, who call Him Father?

When we have received Gods perfect love, we will not fear *(1 John 4:18)*. We will trust, have grace, live in peace, be diligent, walk by faith, keep high moral standards, be patient, kind and godly, *(2 Peter 1:2-9)* after all we will be taking on our Fathers character *(Genesis 1:26-28, Ephesians 4, Colossians 1)*. The more we grow in him and re-train our soul (mind, will and emotions) to line up with the Word of God, the easier it will be for us to love, keep peace and rest in the Finished work of Jesus. Understand we are save by grace through faith and that is not of ourselves or any work or good we have done but it is a gift from God. No one can boast because we all have fallen short of the glory. There is only one way in and that is through Jesus Christ. Our part if we choose to accept Him is to believe. We can only grow into what we have allowed and chosen to believe. Anything we don't believe we cannot have. It is that simple. Religion tries to complicate it and take the power out of it so you won't believe and can't have it. I am telling you. The Word of God is true. You can lean, trust and rely on it. God is on the throne and wants to cover you and take care of you but it is your choice. He will not force himself on anyone and he will respect your choice should you choose to go to hell instead of Heaven. If you would like to receive Jesus as your Lord and Savior say out loud the prayer below that must be prayed in faith believing…

Romans 10:9-10 **If you declare with your mouth, "Jesus is Lord," and believe in your heart that God raised him from the dead, you will be saved. For it is with your heart that you believe and are justified, and it is with your mouth that you profess your faith and are saved.**

Lord Jesus, I ask you to come into my heart. I make you my Lord and Savior. I thank you Jesus for dying on the cross and paying the price for my sins. I believe Jesus was raised from the dead and is seated at the right hand of the Father, ever making intercession for me. Jesus is Lord. Amen *(Romans 8, Ephesians 1:20)*

Chapter Twenty-Six

Decree & Declare

In Christ I am...

Delivered (Psalm 34:19)

In rest (Hebrews 4)

Shame free (Isaiah 49:23)

Protected (Proverbs 30:5)

In perfect peace (Isaiah 26:3, Philippians 4:6-7)

A child of God (1 J0hn 3:1)

The righteousness of God (Isaiah 54:17, Philippians 3:9)

Greatly loved (John 3:16)

Heir according to the promise (Galatians 3:29)

As He is (1 John 4:17)

Provided for (Philippians 4:19)

Carefree (1Peter 5:7)

Strong in the Lord (Ephesians 6:10)

Heir of God and Joint heir with Christ (Romans 8:17)

Full of treasures (Proverbs 8:21)

Eternally Redeemed (Hebrews 9:12)

In Christ I am (continued)…

Led by the Spirit of God (Romans 8:14, John 16:13)

Made perfect (Hebrews 10:1)

Not sin conscience (Hebrews 10:2)

Sanctified (Hebrews 10:10)

Never alone (Hebrews 13:5)

In the Fear of the Lord is…

Knowledge (Proverbs 1:7)

Wisdom (Proverbs 9:10)

Stong confidence (Proverbs 14:26)

Life (Proverbs 14:27)

Refuge (Proverbs 16:26)

Safety (Proverbs 18:10)

I am clean (Proverbs 19:9)

Abide satisfied (Proverbs 19:23)

There are so many other wonderful things that you will learn about yourself and how God made you and what is yours in Christ throughout the bible. Work to get these truths from the Word into the depths of your soul. Come against any and every thought that does not line up with who you are in Christ. Take every thought captive and make it line up with the Word in obedient to Christ.

NOTES

Simple Steps To A Better Life

About the Author

Sandra Williams was born in New Jersey. Having a diversified background, including Italian, German, Chinese and Polish, and all of her great-grandparents being born in their native countries and each having their own rich unique culture, she has learned a balanced perspective as she has grown in American society. She and her husband, Henry, have been married over thirty years and they raised their four boys together. She carries an inner peace despite all life has handed her, including one of her children having leukemia. Through her journey she has gained insight into becoming the best person you can be, having true happiness and keeping the family flourishing. In this book, *Simple Steps to a Better Life,* she shares her insight into the principles of gaining peace, happiness and balance for yourself and passing it on to your family regardless of your stage in life.

For more encouragement you can go to the link below.

https://www.facebook.com/Sandy-Lee-Williams-Simple-Steps-to-a-Better-Life-56913228192/

Simple Steps To A Better Life

www.ingramcontent.com/pod-product-compliance
Lightning Source LLC
Chambersburg PA
CBHW070623300426
44113CB00010B/1633